DIALECTS OF TOURISM

AN INTRODUCTION TO TOURISM AND HOSPITALITY MANAGEMENT

ANAGHA SATHEESAN TM

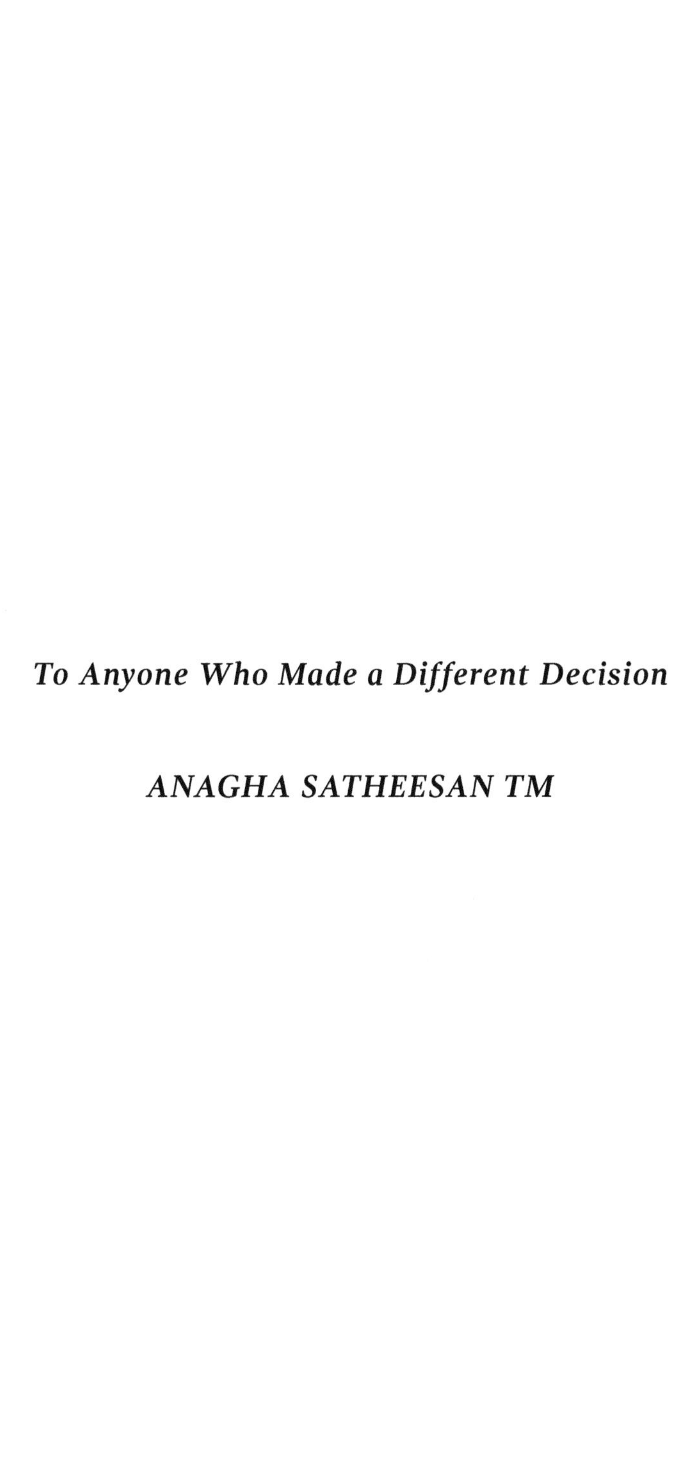

To Anyone Who Made a Different Decision

ANAGHA SATHEESAN TM

Contents

Preface

In an increasingly globalised world and the changing paradigm of urbanised living, the demand for Hospitality and Tourism has increased manifold the world over. Tourism has changed radically in recent years with the onset of many technological and economic changes and an ever-increasing concern for the environment. As well-known, tourism is a social, cultural and economic phenomenon that involves the people's movement to countries or places outside their usual environment, for personal, professional or business purposes. These people are named visitors (and they can be either tourists or day-visitors/ day-travellers residents or non-residents), and tourism refers to their activities, which entail some tourist expenses, as widely admitted by both scholars and specialists. Tourism activities determine certain repercussions on the economy, the natural and built environment, the local population of the destination and the tourists themselves. Thus, multiple impacts are generated, of the range and variety of production factors necessary to create the goods and services purchased by visitors, respectively of the range of agents interested in or affected by tourism; consequently, it is necessary to adopt an integrated approach to tourism development, management and control. This approach is highly recommended for the formulation and implementation of national and local tourism policies, as well as for the establishment of the necessary international agreements or other tourism mechanisms. This book provides a down-to-earth introduction to this complex and multi-faceted industry.

ANAGHA SATHEESAN TM

Acknowledgements

"A sincere attitude of gratitude is a beatitude for secured altitudes. Appreciate what you have been given and you will be promoted higher."

Thank you to each and everyone who lends me physically and mentally to complete this book.

"It's really nice to wake up in the morning realizing that God has given me another day to live. ...

"Thank you, dear God.............

"Thank you, Achan n Amma

"Thank you teachers who conceive and manufacture me........ A good teacher can inspire hope, ignite the imagination, and instil a love of learning."

"Thank you Babi ettaan n Nanooz for indulging me.............

"It's been true in my life that when I've needed a mentor, the right person shows up." Thank you Prasoon ettan for the enlightening thoughts............

"Thank you to all my loving students, friends and family

ANAGHA SATHEESAN TM

CHAPTER ONE

THE PAGES OF HISTORY

"Climb the mountain so you can see the world, not so the world can see you.

~ David McCullough

Tourism is the philosophy and practice of touring, the business of recruiting, accommodating, and entertaining tourists, and the business of operating tours. Tourism can take place both internationally and within the traveller's own country.Tourism is one of the world's fastest-growing industries and a major foreign exchange and employment generation for many countries. It is one of the most remarkable economic and social phenomena. The word 'tour' is derived from the Latin word tornus, meaning 'a tool for making a circle'.Travel is as old as mankind on earth. The man at the beginning of his existence roamed about the surface of the earth in the search of food, shelter, security, and better habitat. However, in course of time, such movements were transformed into wanderlust.

DEFENITION

According to WTO (1993)" Tourism encompasses the activities of persons travelling and staying in places outside their usual environment for not more than one consecutive year for leisure, business, and other purposes."

British Tourism Society (1974) "Tourism is deemed to include any activity concerned with the temporary short-term movement of people to destinations outside the places where they normally live and work, and their activities during the stay at these destinations.

The League of Nations (1937) "A tourist is the individual that spends a period of at least 24 h in a country different than that of residence".

United Nations World Tourism Organization (UNWTO) embarked on a project from 2005 to 2007 to create a common glossary of terms for tourism. It defines tourism as follows:

Tourism is a social, cultural, and economic phenomenon that entails the movement of people to countries or places outside their usual environment for personal or business/professional purposes. These people are called visitors (which may be either tourists or excursionists; residents or non-residents) and tourism has to do with their activities, some of which imply tourism expenditure (United Nations World Tourism Organization, 2008).

Based on the UNWTO definition of tourism, tourism could be categorized as:

- Domestic Tourism: Domestic tourism involves trips made by residents within their own countries.
- International Tourism: International Tourism involves trips between 2 countries. To a certain country, a visit by residents of that country to another country is outbound tourism; a visit to that country by residents of another country is inbound tourism.

EVOLUTION OF TOURISM

In recorded history, there have been instances whereby one can know that man has travelled throughout the ages. It is hard to know when simple travel turned into what we would define as tourism.Tourism is the act and process of spending time away from home in pursuit of recreation, relaxation, and pleasure while making use of the commercial provision of services. As such, tourism is a product of modern social arrangements, beginning in western Europe in the 17th century, although it has antecedents in Classical antiquity.Travel outside a person's local area for leisure was largely confined to wealthy classes, who at times travelled to distant parts of the world, to see great buildings and works of art, learn new languages, experience new cultures, and enjoy pristine nature and taste different cuisines.

Throughout history, people have needed to travel for survival, trade, conquests or curiosity. Very little is known about the prehistoric period between 40000 BC to 10000 BC as no written records exist. But after that period we have records in form of archaeological records, cave paintings, stories, epics etc. The Sumerians invented the wheel around 3500 B.c. The invention of the wheel considerably reduced the burden of travel as also distance. it was now possible to travel hundreds of miles to new lands in search of fortune.

Different tourism experts categorized the development of tourism into 6 stages/

eras and these are as under:

1. The Empire Era (BC to 5th century)
2. The Middle age Era (5th to 14th century)
3. The Renaissance Era (14th to 16th century)
4. The Grand Tour Era (1613 to 1785 A.D)
5. The Mobility Era (1800 to 1944)
6. The Modern Era (1945 to present)

1. The Empire Era (BC to 5th century)

The Empire Era started from the time of the Egyptians to the Greeks and finally Came to an end with the fall of the roman empire. During the time, people began travelling in large numbers for governmental, commercial, educational and religious purposes. Factors that influence people to travel during the Empire era :

- Affluent population with time and money to travel.
- Safe and easy travel.
- Widely accepted currencies.
- Widely used language.
- Legal system which protects personal safety.

2. The Middle age and Renaissance Era (5th to 14th century)

Travel almost disappeared during the Middle Ages when travel became dangerous and sporadic. The travel situation during the Middle Ages :

- Transportation and Safety declined
- Less acceptance of currencies and less knowledge of common languages
- Some travel by crusaders to Holy Lands
- Macro polo's historic travel in the late 13th century
- The rebirth in travel emerged slowly during the Renaissance Era (14th to 16th century)
- Trade routes slowly began to reopen, as commercial activities grew and the merchants ventured into new territories
- Increased interest in travel for commerce and pleasure

3. The Grand Tour Era (1613 to 1785 A.D)

- Trend of luxurious travel started by Wealthy English.
- Developed as a status symbol and spread throughout Europe.
- Goal was to experience the "Civilized World" and study the arts and sciences.
- These travel often lasted for several years.
- Growth in travel for business reasons.

4. The Mobility Era (1800 to 1944)

- Growing economic activity.
- Increase in systems, modes, and speeds of travel (roads, railroads, steamships)
- Thomas Cook (Father of Tourism) developed tour packages for mass travel.
- Invention of the automobile and the aeroplane expanded freedom to travel.
- In 1841, Thomas Cook organized the first tour for a group of 570 to attend a temperance rally in Leicester, England.

5. The Modern Era (1945 to present)

- Paid vacations introduced in the early 1990s made leisure travel possible for the working and middle classes.
- Millions of people were introduced to international travel during world war II.
- Advent of Jet travel shortened travel time.
- Time, money, safety and interest in travel led to the unparalleled growth of tourism.

- Development of mass tourism.
- September 27 is celebrated as world tourism every year. This date was chosen as on that day in 1970, the Statutes of UNWTO were adopted. The purpose of this day is to raise awareness of the role of tourism within the international community.

SIGNIFICANCE OF TOURISM'

As part of the service sector, tourism has become a significant source of revenue for many regions, and even for entire countries. Tourism contributes substantial sums of money to a local economy as a result of payments for products and services required by tourists.

1. Generating Income and Employment

Tourism in India has emerged as an instrument of income and employment generation, poverty alleviation, and sustainable human development.

2. Source of Foreign Exchange Earnings

Tourism is an important source of foreign exchange earnings in India. This has a favourable impact on the balance of payment of the country.

3. Preservation of National Heritage and Environment

Tourism helps preserve several places which are of historical importance by declaring them as heritage sites.

4. Developing Infrastructure

Tourism tends to encourage the development of multiple-use infrastructure that benefits the host community, including various means of transport, health care facilities, and sports centres, in addition to the hotels and high-end restaurants that cater to foreign visitors. The development of infrastructure has in turn induced the development of other directly productive activities.

5. Promoting Peace and Stability

The tourism industry can also help promote peace and stability in developing countries like India by providing jobs, generating income, diversifying the economy, protecting the environment, and promoting cross-cultural awareness. However, key challenges like the adoption of regulatory frameworks, mechanisms to reduce crime and corruption, etc. must be addressed if peace-enhancing benefits from this industry are to be realized.

TRAVEL MOTIVATIONS

There is always a motive behind everything that happens in this world.Motivation is what explains why people or animals initiate, continue or terminate a certain behaviour at a particular time. Tourism is a people-centric and one of the fastest-growing industries. Assessing the behaviour and motivations of tourists is a critical task as the travel decisions of tourists depend on it. Travel has been a nomadic urge in humans earlier in quest of food. As humanity grows the desire for the shelter came into being and with the rise of civilization searched for trade bundles with safety and security. The game-changing moment for mass tourism comes with the rise of leisure time. Assessing the motivations of tourists is a critical task as the travel decisions of tourists depend on it.

MASLOWS NEED HIERARCHY

Abraham Maslow's hierarchy of needs is one of the best-known theories of motivation. Maslow's theory states that our actions are motivated by certain physiological needs. It is often represented by a pyramid of needs, with the most basic needs at the bottom and more complex needs at the top.

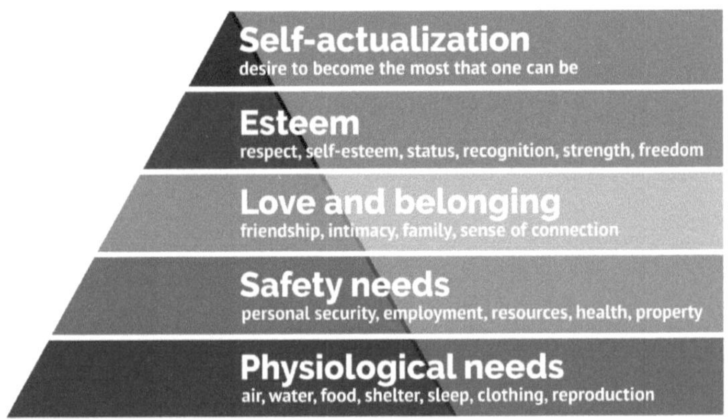

Maslow's hierarchy of needs

TRAVEL MOTIVATION THEORIES

Tourist motivation has been defined "as the global integrating network of biological and cultural forces which gives value and direction to travel choices, behaviour, and experience.". With the gradual expansion of this industry, arose a necessity to assess the factors with vital impact on tourists' motivation to travel.

Understanding and assessing these factors assist service providers to develop the appropriate package for the tourists. Various tourism experts classified travel motivation into;

A. Dann's Theory of Push and Pull Factors

Dann unambiguously explains this theory through two different levels of sociopsychological motivation,

1. Push Factors:

Push factors are socio-psychological as they arise from within the individuals and are associated with factors like yearning for rest, leisure, recreation, spending time with family and friends or even a weekend getaway are all examples of Push factors.

2. Pull factors:

pull factors are largely stimulated by external forces and are destination-specific but they can help set off the push factors. for example, appropriate accommodation, restaurants, entertainment facilities, etc.

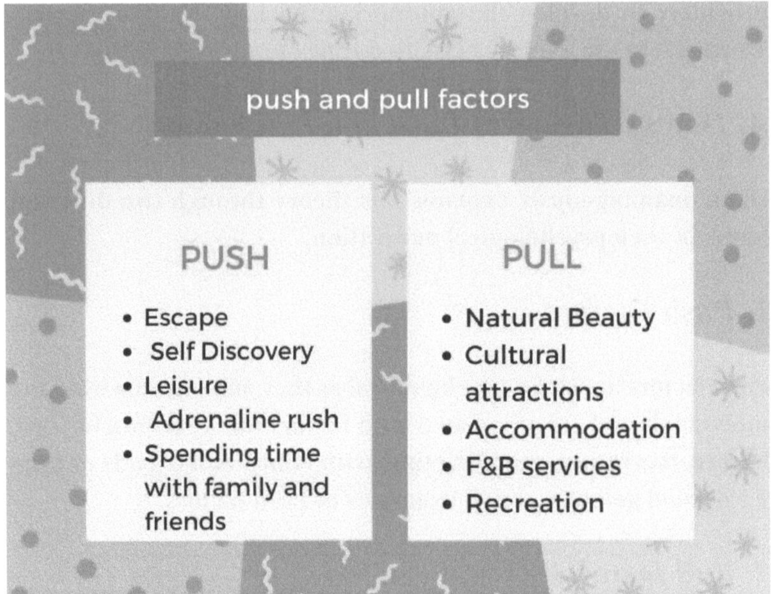

B. Gray's Travel Motivation Theory

Gray's Travel motivation theory constitutes two main motives for travel that is, Wanderlust and Sunlust.

1. Wanderlust

It describes the motive or the desire to go from a known to an unknown place. It is travelling from or leaving a familiar place to go and see different or unfamiliar places. It is about going to different destinations to experience monumental and socio-cultural heritage.

2. Sunlust

Sunlustis related to travel for particular facilities or amenities that do not exist at the place of residence of the tourist. For example, recreation and leisure facilities, shopping, gaming arenas, cultural or historical interest, and many more. Sun-lust also includes travel for adventure activities like trekking, rafting, mountaineering, etc. The duration of this travel is longer-term as compared to wanderlust.

C. McIntosh and Goeldner Categorisation of Travel Motivation

McIntosh and Goeldner (1984) in their theory have summarised all the former studies on travel motivation. They have broadly classified tourist groups into four categories:

1. Physical Motivators

Physical motivators are concerned with health and well-being. It includes rest, sports, and recreational activities like climbing, hiking, swimming, undergoing treatments, attending yoga camps, etc. In short, they are directly related to one's health.

2. Interpersonal Motivators

Human beings are complex social animals that can exchange ideas, thoughts, and values through language or other means of communication. Thus, interpersonal motivators include visiting friends and relatives, spending time with family, etc.

3. Cultural Motivators

The ardent desire to explore ideas, customs, or social behaviour of another community or society falls under this category. For instance, tourists interact with the local community and learn about their dance forms, folklore, history, etc.

4. Status and Prestige Motivators

The need for fame, recognition, respect amongst peers and society, self-fulfilment, ego enhancement, personal development, and desire for the continuation of education are covered under this category. It also includes travel for business or professional purposes

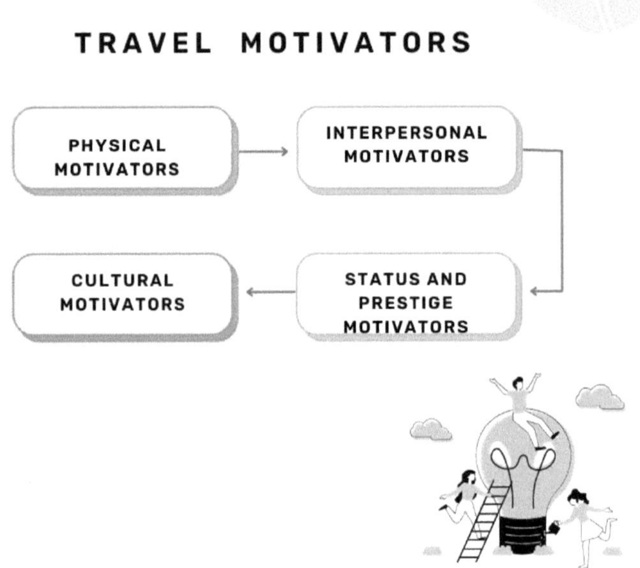

CHAPTER TWO

GROUNDWORKS ON TOURISM

"It's Better to Travel Well than to Arrive"

Buddha

VISITOR, TOURIST, AND EXCURSIONIST

- *Same-day Visitors*

Visitors who do not spend the night in a collective or private accommodation in the country visited. For E.g. cruise ship passengers spend four hours in a port or days-trippers visiting attractions.

- *Tourist*

Visitors who travel to and stay in places outside their usual environment for more than twenty-four (24) hours and not more than one consecutive year for leisure, business and other purposes not related to the exercise of an activity remunerated from within the place visited".

- *Excursionist*

Who visits the place and comes back within 24 hrs at their origin of the destination.

- *Traveller*

Relevant to any movement of a person irrespective of the distance travelled I,e ranging from a small distance of only a few kilometres for seeking of the employment etc.

- *Visitor*

Visiting any country/ destination, performing the exercise of an activity paid from within the place visited greater than 12 months.

- *Transit visitor*

A traveller and a visitor who goes past a country or a place without having a stop or breaking off his journey on the ways other than for layover and consideration/transportation links.

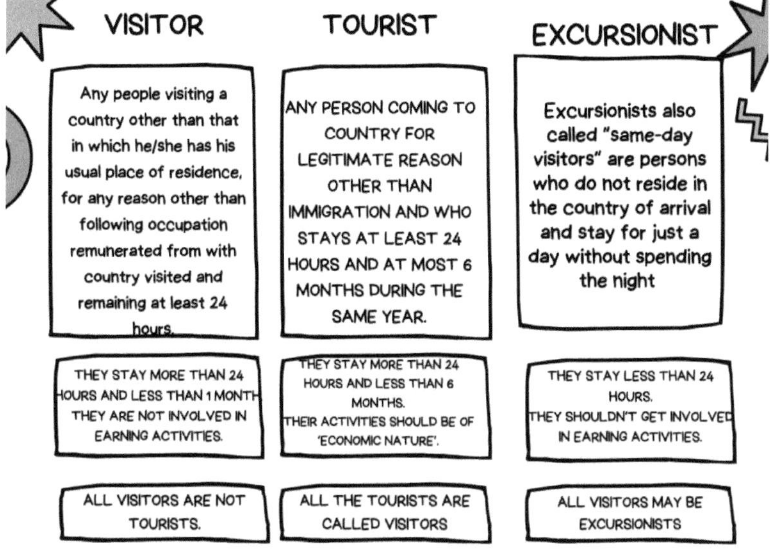

COMPONENTS OF TOURISM

5 A'S

The five vital components of the tourism system are Attraction, Accessibility, Accommodation, Amenities, and Activities.

1. ATTRACTIONS

A tourist attraction is a place of interest that tourists visit, typically for its inherent or exhibited natural or cultural value, historical significance, natural or built beauty, and offering leisure and amusement. Attractions are the main pull factors that draw tourists to travel to the destination. They may be natural or man-made and add to cultural or social aspects of a destination. Attractions are believed to be the greatest influencers of all the components. They can make or break a destination.

Mainly there are two types of attractions:

- Natural Attraction: Natural attractions are places made by nature itself e.g., natural beauty, climate, mountains, landscape, flora and fauna, water resources, beaches, wildlife, caves, safari, etc.
- Man-Made Attraction: Man-made attractions are those Attractions made or developed by humans e.g., monuments, historical buildings, festivals, music, churches, temples, leisure parks, museums, casinos, discos club, etc.

2. ACCESSIBILITY

Accessibility, or transportation, is an important component of the tourist system since it connects the market source and the destination. If there are tourist attractions, travellers must see them. Transportation is not usually a goal, but rather a requirement for the tour's success. However, transportation can sometimes become an attraction.

There are mainly three types of modes of transportation

- Surface transportation: Surface Transportation includes both roadways and railways through the land. It is one of the cheapest means of transportation compared to other modes of transportation.
- Air Transportation: Air Transportation is one of the fastest and costliest means of transportation; air transport is mainly used for travelling to long-distance destinations/places. It has helped a lot, as people can travel long journeys as well as they can travel through high mountains.

- Water Transportation: Water Transportation is one of the oldest modes of transportation through the water. It made an important contribution to travel in the 19th century after the innovation of shipping technology.

3. ACCOMMODATION

Tourist accommodation means any facility consisting of two or more rooms or dwelling units providing lodging and other accommodations to the general public. Accommodation is one of the most crucial aspects of a destination. Any traveller choosing to visit any destination would firstly look for accommodation suited to his/her needs. It should provide him/her food and beverage services, resting facilities, etc. up to his satisfaction level. Accommodation units themselves act as tourist attractions for a large number of people.

Mainly there are two types of accommodation

- Serviced Accommodation: It refers to the services provided by the hotel, resorts, guest houses, motels, boutique hotels, homestay, star category hotels, heritage hotels, lodges, etc. Different hotels are established to provide lodging and food services to guests.
- Self-Catering or Supplementary Accommodation: It refers to the premises which offer accommodation but not the services of a hotel. It provides food and accommodation in return for cash per day. E.g., Youth Hostel, Dharamshalas, Tourist holiday villages, etc.

4. AMENITIES

Amenities include access to basic facilities and services that help a visitor feel comfortable and secure at the destination.

Sometimes referred to as the "pleasantness" of a place, they play an important role in shaping the visitor experience and include things like public restrooms, signage, connectivity, emergency services, postal facilities, roads, sidewalks, safe drinking water, etc. And while it can be tempting to take these elements for granted, ready access to them plays a major role in determining whether visitors will plan a return visit or recommend your destination to others.

5. *ACTIVITIES*

Attractions are often assisted by various activities that enhance the tourist experience. It covers a range of actions a tourist can get involved in a tourist destination such as mountaineering, trekking, rock climbing, caving, camping, fishing, bungee jumping, mountain biking, etc. These activities in tourism have reached great levels owing to enhanced awareness of health and fitness.

TOURISM AS AN INDUSTRY

Tourism has grown in popularity around the world over the years. Tourists require and demand specific facilities and services depending on the nature and purpose of their trip. This has resulted in a wide range of commercial operations that have grown into industries. As a result, travel, and tourism today encompass a wide range of linked industries.

Tourism as a Service industry can be understood as any industry comprising business enterprises that primarily earn money through providing intangible goods or services. Despite the tourism industry being a service industry, it has numerous tangible and intangible elements. Major tangible elements include transportation, accommodation, and other components of the hospitality industry. Major intangible elements relate to the purpose or motivation for becoming a tourist, such as rest, relaxation, the opportunity to meet new people and experience other cultures or simply to do something different and have an adventure.

The tourism industry is linked to the idea of people travelling to other locations, either domestically or internationally, for leisure, social or business purposes. It is closely connected to the hotel industry, the hospitality industry, and the transport industry, and much of it is based around keeping tourists happy, occupied, and equipped with the things they need during their time away from home.

CHAPTER THREE

A FAIRY TALE OF TRANSITS

"Jobs fill your pocket but adventures fill your soul."

~ Jamie Lyn Beatty

Travel and tourism are inseparable. Accessibility is the basic element of tourism; one can't imagine tourism without travel. Transportation is the beginner of tourism business which brings tourists from the place of origin to the place of destination. Accessibility has the capability of converting a normal place into a world-class attraction.The earliest forms of transportation were animals on land and sails on the sea. Travel developed from the need to survive, to expand trade to far-off countries, and the hunger to capture new lands and territories.

The development of new, more efficient, and speedier means of transportation and improved communication facilities have resulted in more travel by people, growth of trade and commerce, and increased volume of traffic. The movement of a large number of people from one place to another, from one country to another, and across the continents have been possible only because of advanced development in means of transportation, such as ships and luxury ocean liners, trains, motorized transport, and aeroplanes. These have made one's individual world smaller in general and now there is no place that one cannot reach quickly and conveniently.

Transportation is vital to tourism. Studies have shown that tourists spend almost 30 to 40 per cent of their total holiday expenditure on transportation and the remaining on food, accommodation, and other activities. This aspect once again highlights the importance of transportation.The various mode of transport can be broadly divided into the following three categories:

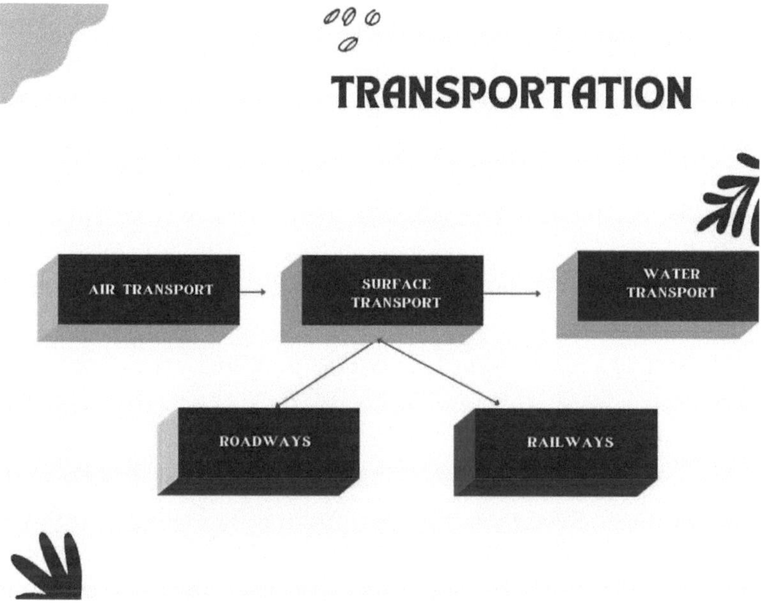

ROAD TRANSPORT

Road transport is one of the most promising and potent means of transportation which can be used for both short-term and long-term travels. Humans travel from place to place in search of food in the primitive era. They tamed animals such as the dog, ox, horse, camel, reindeer, elephants, etc. for carrying the load and travelling. After the discovery of the wheel, humans developed the cart, the chariot, and the carriage.Until the seventeenth century, horses were used for travelling. Later on, better roads were constructed and some of these roads developed into trade routes, which linked many countries. One of them is the Silk Route used to transport silk from China to Persia.

The automobiles provided incomparably greater freedom of travel, choice of destinations, and savings in the time of journey time. A rental car is another aspect of automobile travel that has become a significant sector of the tourism industry.Improvement in road transport facilities stimulates tourism and has a marked influence on the expansion of tourism and the growth of tourist centres. Motor tourists, particularly those from abroad, according to some studies, spend more than non-motoring tourists and bring more benefits to the economy of the area visited by them. With an increase in road traffic and considering tourism requirements, there is a need for proper focus and attention in the overall planning of both tourism and roads.

India has a network of over 6,215,797 kilometres of roads as of 31 March 2020. This is the second-largest road network in the world, after the United States. In the Indian scenario, the road transport sector has expanded manifold in the first fifty years of planned development, both in terms of spread and capacity. It connects the people and places of the country. It links markets, cultural centres, religious places, historical sites, villages, and towns with the national mainstream.

Highways and District roads are primarily used to connect major tourist centres in the country. National Highways (NHS) are principal roads connecting different state capitals to the main cities of the country.According to the Ministry of Roads, Transport and Highways, there are 599 National Highways in India.The National Highways Authority of India (NHAI) and the National Highways and Infrastructure Development Corporation

Limited (NHIDCL) are the nodal agencies responsible for building, upgrading, and maintaining most of the National Highways network. It operates under the Ministry of Road Transport and Highways.

State Highways connect state capitals with district headquarters, important towns, and cities within a state. Major District roads take the traffic from main roads. It contributes significantly to the growth and development of tourism in the country. The availability of district and village roads is promoting rural tourism. The inter-state bus system is well developed

Expressways are high-speed roads that are four- or more lanes and are access controlled where entrance and exit are controlled by the use of ramps that are incorporated into the design of the expressway. Most of the existing expressways in India are toll roads. Expressways make up approximately 2,091 km (1,299 mi) of India's road network, as of 2020

SEA /WATER TRANSPORTATION

"Water is a gift of nature. Human civilization through the gradual application of science and technology has utilized water resources for economic, political and military activities. Remarkable advancements are taking place in water transport due to considerable improvements in the construction, design motive power, speed, and safety of ships and boats.

Water transport is the process of moving people, goods etc. by barge, boat, ship or sailboat over a sea, ocean, lake, canal, river, etc. Humans have been travelling through the water since time immemorial and carried goods and people from one place to another. The boats progressed from the simple raft with some modifications and improvements and were first used around 6000 BC. Travel by ship was the only means of travelling overseas until the middle of the twentieth century.

Inland Waterways comprise rivers, canals and lakes. Naturally navigable rivers are called natural waterways. Canals and canalized rivers belong to the category of 'Artificial Waterways'. Generally, small boats and steamers are operated on rivers to transport people and goods.

During World War I, the operations of the steamship company had to be suspended. After World War II, the large luxury liners again started their operations all over the world. Some of the linear were very large accommodating up to 1000 passengers and had facilities like swimming pools, cinema halls, shops, casinos, etc.

India is endowed with an extensive network of waterways in the form of rivers, canals, backwaters, creeks, and a long coastline accessible through the seas and oceans. It has the largest carrying capacity of any form of transport and is most suitable for carrying bulky goods over long distances.India is the second-largest shipping country in Asia and the sixth-largest in the world. India has a coastline of 6100 km long and only 11 major ports - Mumbai, Kandla, Marmagaon, New Mangalore, Kochi, Chennai, Paradeep, Vishakhapatnam, and Tuticorin.

Despite its length of coastline and several coastal destinations, water transportation for tourists is not very significant. The key concern is its slow speed; for example, the voyage from Kolkata or Chennai to Port Blair takes around 72 hours, which is too long for foreigners.

India has an extensive network of inland waterways in the form of rivers, canals, backwaters, and creeks.Inland water transportation is available in only a few states of India, mainly in Kerala, Gujarat, West Bengal, and Assam. It is difficult for other states to avail of this mode of transport as the rivers are unnavigable most of the time due to the low water depth.

The Inland Waterways Authority of India (IWAI) has identified 111 waterways of India, Of these, only 16 waterways have been declared as National Waterways by the Government of India. These national waterways are maintained by the Inland

Waterways Authority of India (IWAI).

CRUISE INDUSTRY

Cruise ships are large passenger ships used mainly for vacationing. Cruise ships embark on round-trip voyages to various ports of call.where passengers may go on tours known as "shore excursions". On "cruises to nowhere" or "nowhere voyages", cruise ships make two- to three-night round trips without visiting any ports of call. As of December 2018, 314 cruise ships were operating worldwide, with a combined capacity of 537,000 passengers. Cruising has become a major part of the tourism industry, with a greater revenue earning potential.

'Cruise line' is the name given to a company that operates cruise ships and sells cruises to paying customers. Cruising has become a significant tourist industry. Cruise ships act as floating resorts where guests can enjoy amenities and entertainment while being transported along a chain of port calls. Cruise ships are with a complete hospitality staff in addition to the usual ship's crew. It is not uncommon for the most luxurious ships to have more crew and staff than passengers.

ONBOARD FACILITIES

Modern cruise ships typically have aboard some or all of the following facilities:

- Buffet
- restaurant
- Cardroom
- Casino (Only open when the ship is at sea to avoid conflict with local laws)
- Child care facilities
- Cinema
- Clubs

- Fitness centre
- Hot tub
- Indoor and/or outdoor swimming pool with water slides
- Karaoke
- Library
- Lounges
- Observation lounge
- Ping pong tables
- Pool tables
- Shops (Only open when the ship is at sea to avoid merchandising licensing and local taxes)
- Spa
- Teen Lounges
- Theatre with Broadway-style shows

Some ships have bowling alleys, ice skating rinks, rock climbing walls, sky-diving simulators, miniature golf courses, video arcades, ziplines, surfing simulators, water slides, basketball courts, tennis courts, and chain restaurants, ropes obstacle courses, and even roller coaster.

Major cruise ships

1. Wonder of the Seas
2. Symphony of the Seas
3. Harmony of the Seas
4. Allure of the Seas
5. Spectrum of the Seas

RAIL TRANSPORTATION

The railway is the most cost-effective, convenient, and popular means of transportation in the world, especially for long-distance travel. With wooden tracks, the railroad was invented in Germany in the seventeenth century. In the nineteenth and twentieth centuries, railways revolutionised transportation and the mass movement of people.Stockton & Darlington Railway, in England, first railway in the world to operate freight and passenger service with steam traction. The broad-gauge lines account for more than 55 per cent of the total network and carry 85 per cent of total traffic. The steam engines have been replaced by diesel and electric engines which have helped in increasing the speed. Railways have promoted tourism by introducing a special tourist train.

Indian railways provide the principal mode of transportation for the public and tourists. The first rail in India ran between

Bori Bander to Thane (a distance of 35km) on April 16, 1853. Thereafter there was a fast development in the field of railway expansion, up-gradation, and technological development.

Indian Railways (IR) is a statutory body under the ownership of the Ministry of Railways, Government of India that operates India's national railway system. It manages the fourth-largest national railway system in the world by size.It had about 7000 railway stations and runs about 12,000 trains daily.

Indian Railway is an Indian state-owned enterprise, owned and operated by the Government of India through the Ministry of Railways. It is one of the world's largest railway networks comprising 115,000 km and 7,112 stations.

Indian Railways Nationalised in 1951, The country's first railway, built by the Great Indian Peninsula Railway. It is the biggest employer in the world and the largest single undertaking in the country. It has the second biggest electrified system in the world after Russia. Indian Railways is divided into 16 zones which are further sub-divided into 68 divisions.

Indian railway plays an important role in tourism. Journey through trains gives a unique experience. Tourists can see the natural sceneries through trains. Railways connect the major cities of India to popular tourist attractions. A foreigner can experience true India by the riding Indian railway. India railways give an inner view of Indian lifestyles and culture.

LUXURY TRAINS OF INDIA

Ministry of Railways has taken several important initiatives to promote tourism. These include the introduction of new tourist train services on popular tourist circuits in different regions of the country to offer one week's fully packaged rail travel itinerary inclusive of travel, accommodation, onboard catering -on-board and conducted sightseeing tours at the destinations.

1. Palace on Wheels

This luxury tourist train is fully vestibuled, centrally air-conditioned and completely self-sufficient and comprises 14 saloons, 2 dining cars, a Spa car and a lounge car. There are 23 coaches on the train. 104 tourists can travel by train. Each coach is named after former Rajput states and matches the aesthetics and interiors of the royal past. Each coach has four cabins with luxury amenities and Wi-Fi internet. The train has two restaurants, The Mahārāja and The Mahārāni, with a Rajasthani ambience serving continental, Chinese cuisine, one bar-cum-lounge, and a spa.

The train has a 7 night & 8 days itinerary that departs from New Delhi (Day 1) and covers Jaipur (Day 2), Sawai Madhopur and Chittaurgarh (Day 3), Udaipur (Day 4), Jaisalmer (Day 5),

Jodhpur (Day 6), Bharatpur and Agra (Day 7), return to New Delhi (Day 8).

PALACE ON WHEELS — TARRIF

PEAK SEASON		LEAN SEASON	
OCUPANCY TYPE	PRICE PER PERSON	OCCUPANCY TYPE	PRICE PER PERSON
Single Occupancy	USD 8085	Single Occupancy	USD 6615
Double Occupancy	USD 10514	Double Occupancy	USD 8092
Super Deluxe (Suite)	USD 14553	Super Deluxe (Suite)	USD 10920

Fares include accommodation, all meals and non-alcoholic drinks, sightseeing tours, and entrance fees for monuments and palaces.

2. *Deccan Odyssey*

Deccan Odyssey luxury train is one of the ambitious projects of the Indian Railway and Maharashtra State. It is a joint venture between Indian Railways and Govt. of Maharashtra. The objective of running "The Deccan Odyssey" train is primarily to showcase the best tourism assets of Maharashtra and India.

The train reflects the ways of Indian royalty. Each coach is named after some of the best tourist places and forts in Maharashtra. The train has 21 coaches out of which 13 are passenger cars, two presidential suites, one conference car, two dining cars, two generator cars with luggage store, one staff spare car, one spa car, and one bar car.

The train has onboard facilities such as air conditioning, a business centre with internet, FAX, ISD, and STD in the conference car, LCD TV in eleven lounge cars, plasma TV with allied equipment, one health spa car with steam, beauty parlour, and gymnasium, music channel, cell phone on demand, foreign exchange facilities, laundry services, 24 – hour room service, valet attendant, special assistance for physically challenged people, luggage collection facility, guests are provided with arrival kits, fully stocked bar, daily newspapers and magazines, packaged drinking water, and mailbox facilities.

The train has a 7-night & 8 days itinerary. The route begins in Mumbai and travels to Ratnagiri, Sindhudurg, Goa, Kolhapur, Belgaum, Solapur, Aurangabad, Ajanta-Ellora Nasik, and Pune before returning to Mumbai. The fare ranges from USD 7,320 to USD 15,855 according to the type of room and the season.

3. *Fairy Queen*

The Fairy Queen is the oldest working Steam Locomotive in the world, built-in 1855. It was completely overhauled in 1996 & resumed commercial operations in 1997 for 2 Days/1 Nights Tourist circuit from Delhi to Alwar with an overnight stay in Sariska Tiger Reserve, as Fairy Queen train tour In 1998. It was certified as the world's oldest working locomotive by the Guinness Book of World Records.

The Fairy Queen has a 60-seater specially designed air-conditioned chair car with a large glass window from where the passenger can have a frontal view of the locomotive, with a well-maintained pantry car for onboard catering. The coach also has a beautiful lounge in the front, which provides the scenic beauty of the countryside.

4. Golden Chariot

The train, named after the famous Stone Chariot in Hampi, a world heritage site, in Southern India was launched in March 2008. It

comprises 18 thematically designed coaches having passengers Saloons, Restaurants, Bar, Gym, Ayurvedic Centre, Business Centre, etc. with all modern amenities. Its itinerary covers timeless Historical Heritage Sites, Resplendent places, Wildlife, and Golden beaches.

The Golden Chariot offers 3 itineraries:

- Jewels of South

Jewels of South departs Bengaluru and visits Mysore, Hampi, Mahabalipuram, Thanjavur and Chettinad, Cochin, and Kumarakom, returning to Bengaluru.

- Pride of Karnataka

Pride of Karnataka departs Bengaluru and visits Bandipur, Mysore, Halebidu, Chikamgaluru, Hampi, Pattadakal & Aihole, and Goa, returning to Bengaluru.

- Glimpses of Karnataka

Glimpses of Karnataka departs Bengaluru and visits Bandipur, Mysore, and Hampi, returning to Bengaluru.

4. Maharajas‘ Express

The Maharajas’ Express is a luxury tourist train owned and operated by the Indian Railway Catering and Tourism

Corporation (IRCTC). It serves four routes across North-West and Central India, mainly centred on Rajasthan between October and April.

The train comprises 23 carriages which include accommodation, dining, bar, lounge, generator, and store cars. Accommodation is available in 14 guest carriages with a total passenger capacity of 84. The train also has a lounge called the Rajah Club with a private bar, two dining cars, and a dedicated bar car. Maharajas' Express tours operated mainly during the seasons of Oct. to Apr. The fare starts from $5,980 per person. Maharajas Express gives unforgettable memories of the hidden riches of India in its breathtaking beauty and its diversity.

IRCTC

The Indian Railway Catering and Tourism Corporation Limited (IRCTC) is a public sector enterprise under the Ministry of Railways, Government of India. IRCTC was established on 27th September 1999 as an apex body of Indian railway to cater and manage hospitality on railway stations and trains to promote Indian tourism at domestic as well as international levels.

IRCTC headquarter is situated in the heart of the national capital New Delhi. To operate the operations smoothly five zonal offices are working in Delhi, Kolkata, Mumbai, Chennai & Secunderabad. IRCTC provides complete travel and tourism solutions for the various customer segments and also caters to trains and stations over the Indian Railway network. It is also called the "Lifeline of the nation".

AIR TRANSPORTATION

Air travel is the process of going from place to place by any flying object, such as aeroplanes, helicopters, balloons, or anything that can fly. The dream of human flight must have begun with the observation of birds soaring through the sky. On December 17, 1903, Orville and Wilbur Wright capped four years of research and design efforts with a 120-foot, 12-second flight at Kitty Hawk, North Carolina - the first powered flight in a heavier-than-air machine. Before that, people had flown only in balloons and gliders.

The use of air travel has greatly increased in recent decades – worldwide it doubled between the mid-1980s and the year 2000. Modern air travel is much safer than road travel. Air travel can be separated into two general classifications: national/domestic and international flights. Domestic flights are flights that take you from one location to another within the same country. International flights are flights that connect points inside one country to points within another country. Domestic and international flights are available for private or public travel.

An airline is a company that provides air transport services for travelling passengers and freight.An airport is a complex of runways and buildings for the take-off, landing, and maintenance of civil aircraft, with facilities for passengers. Airlines traditionally have three travel classes, First Class, Business Class, and Economy Class.

International air travel is governed by the International Air Transport Association (IATA). IATA is made up of more than 105 major airlines from around the world. The International Air Transport Association (IATA) sets ticket prices for various modes of transportation around the world. Domestic fares are set by the relevant government. In most cases, airfares are set based on the volume and demand for air travel in a given area.

Air transport in India made a beginning in 1911 when airmail operation commenced over a little distance of 10 km between Allahabad and Naini. But its real development took place in the post-Independent period.

Air India is India's national flag carrier and plays a major role in connecting India with the rest of the world. India will be the third-largest civil aviation market in the world by 2020. In the Indian scenario, India's booming economy has created a large middle-class population that can now afford air travel.

The Airport Authority of India is responsible for providing safe, efficient air traffic and aeronautical communication services in the Indian Air Space.

The Ministry of Civil Aviation (MoCA) of the Government of India is the nodal Ministry responsible for the formulation of national policies and programs for the development and regulation of civilian aviation, and for devising and implementing schemes for the orderly growth and expansion of civilian air transport. The Directorate General of Civil Aviation (DGCA) is the national regulatory body for civil aviation under the Ministry of Civil Aviation. This directorate investigates aviation accidents and incidents.

The airline industry has changed very fast due to many reasons like the introduction of low-cost airlines, a greater number of flights, computerization of the airline sector, and better marketing. Regular flights are available from all major cities of India. Recently, honourable Prime Ministry Sri Narendra Modi has announced flights from India to Sri Lanka keeping in mind Buddhist tourists. Air transportation is one of the most important modes of transportation for tourists across the world.T oo meet the increasing demand and improve the travel experience, airline companies are adding new aircraft to their fleets like Choppers, Air Taxies, Boeings, etc. Also, they are developing airports, opening new airports, and using innovative technologies. Because of the matchless role of airlines for long distances, the aviation industry is developing very fast.

CHAPTER FOUR

TRAVEL INSTRUMENTS

"Live your life by a compass, not a clock."

– Stephen Covey

TRAVEL DOCUMENTS

A travel document refers to an identification document issued by a government or an organization to facilitate the movement of individuals across country borders. Travel documents usually assure other governments that the bearer may return to the issuing country, and are often issued in booklet form to allow other governments to place visas as well as entry and exit stamps into them. The most common travel document is a passport, which usually gives the bearer more privileges like visa-free access to certain countries. Border control policies typically require travellers to present valid travel documents to ascertain their identity, nationality, or permanent residence status, and eligibility to enter a given jurisdiction.Different countries impose varying travel document regulations and requirements as part of their border control policies. The most commonly required travel documents are as follows:

A. Passport

A passport is an official travel document issued by a government that contains a given person's identity. It enables its holder to travel to and from foreign countries and to access consular assistance while overseas. The document certifies the personal identity and nationality of its holder. Standard passports contain the full name, photograph, place, date of birth, signature, and expiration date of the passport. While passports are typically issued by national governments, certain subnational governments are authorized to issue passports to citizens residing within their borders.

An Indian passport is issued by the Ministry of External Affairs of the Republic of India to Indian citizens for international travel. It enables the bearer to travel internationally and serves as proof of Indian citizenship as per the Passports Act (1967).

There are three types of passports available in India are –

- Ordinary Passport (Dark Blue cover) is issued to ordinary citizens for private travel, such as for vacation, study, and business trips (36 or 60 pages). It is a "Type P" passport, where P stands for Personal.
- Official Passport (White cover) is issued to individuals representing the Government of India on official business, including members of the Indian Armed Forces stationed abroad. It is a "Type S" passport, S stands for Service
- Diplomatic Passport (Maroon cover) is issued to Indian diplomats, Members of Parliament, members of the Union Council of Ministers, certain high-ranking government officials, and diplomatic couriers, as well as their dependents. Upon request, it may also be issued to high-ranking state-level officials travelling on official business. It is a "Type D" passport, with D standing for Diplomatic.

B. VISA

A visa is a conditional authorization granted by a polity to a foreigner that allows them to enter, remain within, or leave its territory. A visa is often a document, a seal, or a stamp on a passport that grants the holder of that passport, entry, exit, and stay in a foreign country for a specific period. Some passports will grant visa-free movement into and out of some countries.

Visa applications in advance of arrival give countries a chance to consider the applicant's circumstances, such as financial security, the reason for travel, and details of previous visits to the country. Visitors may also be required to undergo and pass security or health checks upon arrival at the port of entry.Visas can also be *single-entry*, which means the visa is cancelled as soon as the holder leaves the country; *double-entry*, or *multiple-entry*, which permits double or multiple entries into the country with the same visa. Countries may also issue re-entry permits that allow temporarily leaving the country without invalidating the visa. Even a business visa will normally not allow the holder to work in the host country without additional work permit centres.

1. Transit visas

For passing through the country of issue to a destination outside that country. The validity of transit visas is usually limited by short terms such as several hours to ten days depending on the size of the country or the circumstances of a particular transit itinerary.

2. visitor visas

For short visits to the visited country.

3. Employment Visa

Highly skilled Individuals intending to take up employment

4. Business Visa

Visiting India for a business purpose

5. Student visa

which allows its holder to study at an institution of higher learning in the issuing country.

6. Medical Visa

For seeking medical treatment outside one own country, at recognized and specialized hospitals and treatment centres

7. Residence visa

Granted to people obtaining long-term residence in the host country.

8. Dependent visa

Issued to certain family members of the holder of a long-stay visa

9. On-arrival visas

Also known as visas on arrival (VOA), they are granted at a port of entry. This is distinct from visa-free entry, where no visa is required, as the visitor must still obtain the visa on arrival before proceeding to immigration control.

10. Schengen visa

A Schengen visa is a short stay visa allowing its holder to circulate in the Schengen area. The Schengen area covers 26 countries ("Schengen States") without border controls between them. These countries are Austria, Belgium, the Czech Republic, Denmark, Estonia, Finland, France, Germany, Greece, Hungary, Iceland, Italy, Latvia, Liechtenstein, Lithuania, Luxembourg, Malta, the Netherlands, Norway, Poland, Portugal, Slovakia, Slovenia, Spain, Sweden and Switzerland.

C. VACCINATION

From Covid 19 to Ebola, travelling has always contributed to the spread of the deadliest pandemics. Whatever the destination, the best possible pre-travel preparation is essential to protect the health of travellers while away. There are two types of immunizations, which are compulsory and recommended. Compulsory vaccinations are only required by certain countries. Some countries may recommend certain immunizations, especially when the traveller normally travels outside the urban areas. The travellers should therefore be advised to obtain a health certificate, proving that they have been vaccinated for a specified infectious disease. If they are not able to produce the same, they could be deported back out of the country or they could be detained and kept in quarantine.

The WHO international certificate of vaccination can usually be obtained from health clinics, doctors, and health authorities. For the certificate of vaccination to be valid, it must bear the name of vaccination, and the date, and should be signed by the concerned authorities in the country of issue. Cholera and yellow fever are the only vaccinations that are normally required for travelling to certain countries. Various schemes for health passports or vaccination certificates have been proposed for people who have been vaccinated against COVID-19.

D. TRAVEL INSURANCE

Travel insurance is an insurance product for covering unforeseen losses incurred while travelling, either internationally or domestically. Basic policies generally only cover emergency medical expenses while overseas, while comprehensive policies typically include coverage for trip cancellation, lost luggage, flight delays, public liability, and other expenses.

Travel insurance is risk-based and takes into account a range of factors to determine whether a traveller can purchase a policy and what the premium will be. This generally includes destination countries or regions, the duration of the trip, the age of the travellers, and any optional benefits that require coverage. Most travel insurance policies must be purchased before departure from home, or at the first departure point.

CHAPTER FIVE

TRAVEL PRODUCTS

"I am not a great book, I am not a great artist, but I love art and I love food, so I am the perfect traveller."

– Michael Palin

TOURISM PRODUCTS

A product is anything that is manufactured and available for sale. A tourism product can be defined as the sum of the physical and psychological satisfaction it provides to tourists during their travelling en route to the destination. The tourist product focuses on facilities and services designed to meet the needs of the tourist.

Tourism products can be studied from two different perspectives i.e., from the perspective of the suppliers (sellers) and that of the consumers (tourists). Services produced by suppliers may range from transportation, lodging, food and beverages, entertainment facilities, and so on. Similarly, tourists or consumers may demand the products based on their satisfying needs such as attraction, amenities, and accessibility. Further such needs may be categorized based on tourists' participation and use of natural resources of a country. While supplier-based categorization will be studied as part of tourism systems, this unit will focus on consumers' participation in natural resources and typology based on such participation.

TYPES OF TOURISM PRODUCTS

1. Natural Tourism Products

The tourism products which have been created using the resources provided by nature are called natural tourism products. Natural tourism products are closely associated with the natural environment. The natural settings in such tourism products attract tourists towards them.Major natural tourism resources could be:

- Scenic attractions
- Mountains
- Glaciers
- Climate
- Caves
- Deserts
- Sea beaches
- Islands
- Rivers
- Lakes
- Waterfalls
- Wildlife
- Forests
- Flora and fauna

These natural resources are utilized and developed to present them as tourism products. Basic infrastructure like transport, accommodation, and food is provided at such places to convert them into products.

2. Manmade Tourism Products

These are those tourism products that have been built or created by humans to satisfy the leisure, pleasure, or business needs of the tourists. Human beings over centuries have created facilities for the comfort of living. Such creations are natural manifestations of human endeavour in the process of evolution. Such manifestations, elegant structures, or facilities by creative humans become attractions common in the civilization. These products include not only core attractions but also facilities and services that have made a mark in themselves and have become attractions for most. Major man-made tourism products could be:

- Historical monuments
- Historical sites
- Fairs and festivals
- Customs and traditions
- Cuisines
- Museums
- Art galleries
- Folk dances
- Handicrafts
- Religious centres
- Adventure activities
- Resorts
- Botanical gardens and zoos
- Recreational and Shopping facilities.

3. Symbiotic Tourism Product

Apart from pure natural and man-made products, there are some types of products that are a blend of both natural and man-made features. In such products, nature remains the core resource on which humans create recreational facilities. Nature provides the resource and man adds certain facilities to convert them into a tourism product. Thus, such products are called creations by the symbiosis of nature and man.

For example, the water adventure activities in Goa have been created by humans whereas the resource on which these activities are performed has been provided by nature which is the sea. Other examples of such products could be wildlife sanctuaries, marine parks, and national parks. However, the core attraction is such products usually remain natural. While creating symbiotic tourism products it is always taken into consideration that we do not overexploit the natural resources and always use them to an acceptable limit. Such products are managed by human beings by taking care of natural beauty as far as possible.

CHARACTERISTICS OF TOURISM PRODUCTS

1. INTANGIBLE

Tourism is an intangible product means tourism is such a kind of product that cannot be touched or seen, But the facilities are available for a specified time and specified use. When we buy a tourism product, say a tour package we buy a dream, a concept or an idea. We cannot touch it, feel it or smell it. Whenever we plan a trip we start imagining what we will see at the destination. When we reach the destination only then do we realize the level of satisfaction or the value of money that we have got in return. In this way, tourism products are said to be intangible.

2. Heterogeneity

Tourism is a service industry. In this industry humans serve humans. In providing tourism-related services human element is always involved which ultimately makes the standardization of these services a very difficult task. For example, at a destination, in a hotel, the front office executive greeting the tourist with a smiling face and politeness will make the tourist feel happy about the services of the hotel and will carry good memories with him about the destination. On the other hand, some other day, in the same hotel if the same front office executive behaves rudely and does not do his job smilingly and politely will give a bad impression about the services of the hotel.

3. Inseparability

Inseparability means the product/service cannot be separated from the original service provider.Most travel products are first sold and then produced and consumed at the same time. This is an aspect that sets tourism apart from tangible products. When you buy a new computer, it is produced and shipped before you see it on the website or at the retailer's premises. The consumption of that computer – using it – takes place after purchase at your home. You cannot take the hotel room home – only the small bottles of shampoo and toothpaste. And you cannot enjoy the alpine sleigh ride in your living room. Tourism products can only be consumed at the supplier's premises.

4. Perishability

Tourism products are said to be highly perishable. It means that this product cannot be stored for a long time like other consumer products. A simple consumer product says a bar of soap is produced in factories and is made available at the shops for selling to prospective buyers. If unsold, it can remain there for a long time even days and months. However, an unsold room in a hotel or an empty seat in transport is lost forever. This is because in tourism products the production and the consumption take place at the same time. Production takes place only when the customer is present. And once the consumption starts it cannot be stopped, interrupted or modified. If a tourism product is not used it gets lost for that time. Tourism is highly dependent on seasons and due to perishability characteristics, the accommodation and transport sectors offer high discounts during off-seasons.

5. Ownership

In the case of consumer products, we go to the market, pay the price and bring the product back with us. In the case of tourism products and services we pay for their use and can never become their owners. At a destination, we pay for the accommodation and use it but we do not become the owner of the hotel. Similarly, we pay for the air seat but never own it. The non-ownership of services transfers only the right to use the services for a limited time.

CHAPTER SIX

BREEDS OF TOURISM

The Roots of Education Are Bitter, But The Fruit Is Sweet

~~Aristotle

ECOTOURISM

According to The International Ecotourism Society (TIES), ecotourism can be defined as "responsible travel to natural areas that conserve the environment, sustains the well-being of the local people, and involves interpretation and education". Such travelling can be created thanks to an international network of individuals, institutions, and the tourism industry where tourists and tourism professionals are educated on ecological issues.

Ecotourism attracts people who wish to interact with the environment and, in varying degrees, develop their knowledge, awareness, and appreciation of it. Thenmala is India's first planned Ecotourism destination and was selected by the World Tourism Organisation as a premier eco-friendly project.

CHARACTERISTICS OF ECO-TOURISM

Ecotourism is travel to fragile, pristine, and usually protected areas that strive to be low impact and (often) small scale. It helps educate the traveller, provides funds for conservation, directly benefits the economic development and political empowerment of local communities, and fosters respect for different cultures and human rights.

Some important characteristics of ecotourism are the following:

1. Involves travel to the natural destination.

These destinations are often remote areas, whether inhabited or uninhabited, and are usually under some kind of environmental protection for national, international, communal, or private travel.

2. Minimize impact.

Tourism has a negative impact. Ecotourism aims to reduce the negative effects of hotels, trails, and other infrastructure by utilising recycled or readily accessible local building materials, renewable energy sources, trash and rubbish recycling and safe disposal, and environmentally and culturally sensitive architectural design.

3. Builds environmental awareness

Ecotourism means education, for both tourists and residents of nearby communities. Well before the tour begins, tour operators should supply travellers with reading material about the country, environment, and local people, as well as a code of conduct for both the traveller and the industry itself. Ecotourism projects should also help educate members of surrounding communities, schoolchildren, and the broader public in the host country.

4. Provides direct financial benefits for conservation

Ecotourism helps raise funds for environmental protection, research, and education through a variety of mechanisms, including park entrance fees; tour company, hotel, airline, and airport taxes. And voluntary contributions.

5. Provides financial benefits and empowerment for local people

Ecotourism holds that national parks and other conservation areas will survive only if, there are happy people around the perimeters. The local community must be involved with and receive income and other tangible benefits (potable water, roads, health clinics, etc.) from the conservation area and its tourist facilities.

6. Respects local culture

Ecotourism is not only "greener" but also less culturally intrusive and exploitative than conventional tourism. Whereas prostitution, black markets, and drugs often are by-products of mass tourism, ecotourism strives to be culturally respectful and the human population of a host country.

7. Supports human rights and democratic movements

The United Nations-sponsored World Tourism Organization proclaims that tourism contributes to "international understanding, peace, prosperity, and universal respect for and observance of human rights and fundamental freedoms for all.

MAJOR ECOTOURISM DESTINATION

- Kerala: Munnar, Backwater waterways, Thenmala, Thodupuzha, Eravikulam National Park, Periyar National Park, Kodaikanal.
- Karnataka: Coorg, Nagarhole, Nagarhole National Park, Bandipur National Park.
- Goa: Galgibaga Beach.
- Andhra Pradesh: Tyda, Maredumilli.
- Odisha: Chilika.

ADVENTURE TOURISM

Adventure tourism is a new concept in the tourism industry. The tourism industry adopted adventure tourism, but there is not any specific definition of adventure tourism. Adventure travel is a leisure activity that takes place in an unusual, exotic, remote, or wilderness destination. It tends to be associated with high levels of activity by the participant, most of it outdoors.

Adventure travellers expect to experience various levels of risk, excitement, and tranquillity and be personally tested. In particular, they are explorers of unspoiled, exotic parts of the planet and also seek personal challenges. The main factor distinguishing adventure tourism from all other forms of tourism is the planning and preparation involved.

According to the Adventure Travel Trade Association, “adventure tourism is a tourist activity that includes physical activity, cultural exchange, or activities in nature.”

Canadian Tourism Commission 1995 defines adventure tourism as, “an outdoor leisure activity that takes place in an unusual, exotic, remote or wilderness destination, involves some form of unconventional means of transportation, and tends to be associated with low or high levels of activity.”

TYPES OF ADVENTURE TOURISM

In recent years, adventure tourism has exploded around the world, with tourists exploring previously unknown areas. This enables a new destination to portray itself as unique, appealing to traveller travellers as a once-in-a-lifetime experience.

Adventure tourism includes various activities like caving, hiking, sailing, trekking, etc. Adventure tourism is categorized into two categories. These are the following:

1. Hard Adventure

Hard adventure refers to high-risk activities that necessitate a high level of dedication and advanced abilities. Hard tourism includes the activities like climbing mountains/rock/ice, trekking, caving, etc.

Hard adventure activities are highly risky in net activities and necessitate the use of a professional guide with advanced expertise. Many tourists died while climbing mountains and caving on a irregularly

Hard adventure activities are highly risky and dangerous in net activities are the following as:

- Caving
- Mountain Climbing
- Rock Climbing
- Ice Climbing
- Trekking
- Sky Diving

2. Soft Adventure

Soft adventure refers to activities that have a high perceived risk but low actual risk, require little commitment and basic abilities and are usually led by skilled guides. Backpacking, camping, hiking, kayaking, and other forms of soft tourism are examples.

In nature, soft adventure activities are low-risk. Professional guides lead these activities. Soft adventure is a popular adventure tourism category. Soft adventure excursions account for almost 25% of all trips taken from North America and Europe.

These activities are less dangeroudangerousared to hard adventure activities. These activities are always led by professional guides. These activities are following as:

- Backpacking
- Birdwatching
- Camping
- Canoeing
- Eco-tourism
- Fishing
- Hiking
- Horseback riding
- Hunting
- Kayaking/sea/Whitewater
- Orienteering
- Safaris
- Scuba Diving
- Snorkelling
- Skiing
- Snowboarding
- Surfing

MAJOR ADVENTURE TOURISM DESTINATIONS

- Manali: Solang Valley, Rohtang Pass and Old Manali.

- Kaziranga: Assam, take an elephant safari and spot rhinos and other wildlife.
- Lahaul-Spiti: Himachal Pradesh, a picturesque mountain terrain
- Pokhara: A Nepalese khukuri, carpets and handicrafts
- Rishikesh: Uttarakhand, engage in activities such as rafting in the Ganga River, rock and cliff climbing bungee jumping.

SUSTAINABLE TOURISM

In the broadest sense, sustainability refers to the ability to maintain or support a process continuously over time.The World Commission on Environment and Development (The Brundtland Commission) brought the term 'sustainable tourism development' into common use in its seminal report (1987) called 'Our Common Future.'

"Sustainable Development is the development that meets the needs of the present without compromising the ability of future generations to meet their own needs." Sustainable tourism is the form of tourism that meets the needs of tourists, the tourism industry, and host communities today without compromising the ability of future generations to meet their own needs, which is economically viable but does not destroy the resources on which the future of tourism will depend, notably the physical environment and the social fabric of the host community.

The World Tourism Organization defines sustainable, "Sustainable tourism development meets the needs of present tourists and host regions while protecting and enhancing opportunities for the future. It is envisaged as leading to management of all resources in such a way that economic, social and aesthetic needs can be fulfilled while maintaining cultural integrity, essential ecological processes, biological diversity, and life support systems."

PRINCIPLES OF SUSTAINABLE TOURISM

Tourism Concern, 1991 in association with the Worldwide Fund for Nature (WWF) gives 10 principles for sustainable tourism. These are the following:

1. Using resources sustainably.

Conservation and sustainable use of natural, social, and cultural resources are critical and profitable in the long run.

2. Reducing over-consumption and waste.

Reducing overconsumption and waste reduces the costs of repairing long-term environmental damage while also improving tourism quality.

3. Maintaining biodiversity.

Maintaining and encouraging ecological, social, and cultural variety is critical for long-term tourist sustainability and ensures the industry's durability.

4. Integrating tourism into planning

Tourism development which is integrated into a national and local strategic planning framework and which undertakes environmental impact assessments increases the long-term viability of tourism.

5. Supporting local economies

Tourism that supports a wide range of local economic activities and which takes environmental costs and values into account, both protects these economies and avoids environmental damage.

6. Involving local communities.

Local communities' full participation in the tourist sector benefits not only them and the environment in general, but it also increases the quality of the tourism experience.

7. Consulting stakeholders and the public.

If the tourism sector and local communities, organizations, and institutions are to work together and overcome any conflicts of interest, they must engage with each other.

8. Training staff

The quality of the tourism product is improved via staff training that incorporates sustainable tourism into work practices, as well as the recruitment of workers at all levels.

9. Marketing tourism responsibly

Marketing that provides tourists with full and responsible information increases respect for the natural, social and cultural environments of destination areas and enhances customer satisfaction.

10. Undertaking research.

Constant industry research and monitoring, related to the quality data collection and analysis, is critical to assisting in the resolution of challenges and bringing advantages to destinations, the industry, and consumers.

RESPONSIBLE TOURISM

Responsible Tourism is about "making better places for people to live in and better places for people to visit." Responsible Tourism requires that operators, hoteliers, governments, local people, and tourists take responsibility, and take action to make tourism more sustainable.

Responsible Tourism was defined in Cape Town in 2002 alongside the World Summit on Sustainable Development. In Cape Town, the delegates from twenty countries around the world included people from all spheres related directly or indirectly to the tourism industry, right from tour operators, airlines, and hotel groups to national parks, government, and conservation authorities. They called upon all involved to develop guidelines to ensure the social, economic, and environmental protection of places where tourists visit.

The World Travel Market has adopted the Cape Town Declaration definition of Responsible Tourism for its World Responsible Tourism Day which encourages the industry to take responsibility for making tourism more sustainable and demonstrate their responsibility.

The Cape Town Declaration recognises that Responsible Tourism takes a variety of forms, it is characterised by travel and tourism which:

- Minimises negative economic, environmental, and social impacts;
- Generates greater economic benefits for local people and enhances the well-being of host communities, improves working conditions and access to the industry;
- Involves local people in decisions that affect their lives and life changes;
- Makes positive contributions to the conservation of natural and cultural heritage, to the maintenance of the world's diversity;

• Provides more enjoyable experiences for tourists through more meaningful connections with local people, and a greater understanding of local cultural, social, and environmental issues;

• Provide access for people with disabilities and the disadvantaged;

• It is culturally sensitive, engenders respect between tourists and hosts, and builds local pride and confidence.

NATURE-BASED TOURISM

Nature Tourism is Responsible for travel to natural areas, which conserves the environment and improves the welfare of local people. Most nature-based tourism destinations are located in protected areas that attract large numbers of visitors.From the standpoint of conservation, nature-based tourism provides incentives for local communities and landowners to conserve wildlife habitats upon which the industry depends. As nature tourism becomes more important to the local economy, communities have additional incentives to conserve their remaining natural areas for wildlife and wildlife enthusiasts.

Nature-based tourism activities represent high-level adventure activities like jet boating, skydiving, and mountain climbing as well as more relaxing activities like bush walking, wildlife and scenic tours, and boat cruises. It is the most known type of tourism which every country has. Governments and international organizations, especially those related to nature and environmental protection, are always concerned about increasing community awareness of protecting and preserving nature and setting laws and regulations that keep nature safe. Birdwatching, photography, stargazing, camping, hiking, hunting, fishing, and park touring are some great examples of nature-based tourism.

GREEN TOURISM

The concept of green tourism has evolved and is presently used with different meanings. The original one, spread during the 1980s, stands for small-scale tourism which involves visiting natural areas while minimizing environmental impacts. In this line, green tourism has been used interchangeably with such concepts as ecotourism, nature tourism, and rural tourism.

International organizations have defined the notion in line with the concept of sustainable tourism, which also considers other dimensions than environmental protection. In fact, for the World Tourism Organization, green tourism consists of "tourism activities that can be maintained, or sustained, indefinitely in their social, economic, cultural and environmental contexts".

Businesses have generally adopted a broader meaning for green tourism that is, any tourism activity operating in an environmentally friendly manner. However, more and more lately, green tourism has been oftentimes used by businesses that do not put that much effort into making their activity more sustainable and the term became more known for greenwashing. Greenwashing refers to companies that are more interested in becoming known for their green tourism and less for their contribution to the environment and local communities.

CHAPTER SEVEN

LINE OF ART IN TOURISM

"Travel far enough, you meet yourself."

- David Mitchell

CULTURAL TOURISM

Cultural tourism is a type of tourism activity in which the visitor's essential motivation is to learn, discover, experience, and consume the tangible and intangible cultural attractions/ products in a tourism destination.

According to the definition adopted by the UNWTO General Assembly, at its 22nd session (2017), Cultural Tourism implies "A type of tourism activity in which the visitor's essential motivation is to learn, discover, experience and consume the tangible and intangible cultural attractions/products in a tourism destination. These attractions/products are related to a set of distinctive material, intellectual, spiritual and emotional features of a society that encompasses arts and architecture, historical and cultural heritage, culinary heritage, literature, music, creative industries, and the living cultures with their lifestyles, value systems, belief,s and traditions".

CULTURAL TOURISM ACTIVITIES

- Staying with a local family in a homestay
- Having a tour around a village or town
- Learning about local employment, for example through a tour of a tea plantation or factory
- Undertaking volunteer work in the local community
- Taking a course such as cooking, art, embroidery, etc
- Visiting a museum
- Visiting a religious building, such as a Mosque
- Socialising with members of the local community
- Visiting a local market or shopping area
- Trying the local food and drink
- Going to a cultural show or performance
- Visiting historic monuments

HEALTH TOURISM

Health tourism covers those types of tourism which have as a primary motivation, the contribution to physical, mental, and/or spiritual health through medical and wellness-based activities which increase the capacity of individuals to satisfy their own needs and function better as individuals in their environment and society.

Health tourism is the umbrella term for the subtypes: wellness tourism and medical tourism.

Medical tourism is a type of tourism activity that involves the use of evidence-based medical healing resources and services (both invasive and non-invasive). This may include diagnosis, treatment, cure, prevention, and rehabilitation.

Wellness tourism is a type of tourism activity that aims to improve and balance all of the main domains of human life including physical, mental, emotional, occupational, intellectual, and spiritual. The primary motivation for wellness tourism is to engage in preventive, proactive, lifestyle-enhancing activities such as fitness, healthy eating, relaxation, pampering, and healing treatments

REASONS FOR MEDICAL TOURISM

- Disappointment with medical treatment at home.
- Lack of access to health care at a reasonable cost and, time.
- Inadequate insurance and income to pay for local healthcare.
- The rise of high-quality medical care in developing countries.
- Greater mobility.
- A wish to get medical services away from the common environment (escapism).
- The growing popularity of getting medical services abroad.
- No wait-list.
- Accesses to the latest technology.

International healthcare accreditation is the process of certifying a level of quality for healthcare providers and programs across multiple countries. International healthcare accreditation organizations certify a wide range of healthcare programs such as hospitals, primary care centres, medical transport, and ambulatory care services. There are several accreditation schemes available based in many different countries around the world.

Medical tourism carries some risks that locally provided medical care either does not carry or carries to a much lesser degree.Medical tourism is a growing sector in India. India is becoming the 2nd medical tourism destination after Thailand. Chennai is regarded as "India's Health City" as it attracts 45% of health tourists visiting India and 40% of domestic health tourists.

RURAL TOURISM

UNWTO understands Rural Tourism as "a type of tourism activity in which the visitor's experience is related to a wide range of products generally linked to nature-based activities, agriculture, rural lifestyle/culture, angling, and sightseeing.

Rural Tourism activities take place in non-urban (rural) areas with the following characteristics:

i) low population density

ii) landscape and land-use dominated by agriculture and forestry

iii) traditional social structure and lifestyle".

Rural tourism showcases the rural life, art, culture, and heritage at rural locations, thereby benefiting the local community economically and socially as well as enabling interaction between the tourists and the locals for a more enriching tourism experience.

IMPORTANCE AND BENEFITS OF RURAL TOURISM

Rural tourism is an important form of the tourism sector which plays an important role and gives many benefits to rural areas and communities. When tourists travel to rural areas, they support the local economy and help variously. Rural tourism helps in the development of rural areas and the living standards of host communities.

Some importance and benefits of rural tourism are the following:

- Provides a source of new, alternative or supplementary income and employment in rural areas.

- Rural tourism spurs infrastructure development in rural areas.
- Help to reduce gender and other social power
- Encourage collective community
- Reinvigorate local culture.
- Instill the sense of local pride, self-esteem, and identity
- Contribution to conservation and protection.
- Increase the living standards of the local community.
- Assists refurbishment and re-use of abandoned properties.
- Provide opportunities for retaining population in areas that might otherwise experience depopulation.
- Enable areas to be repopulated.

ETHNIC TOURISM

Ethnic Tourism is the tourists' interest in the customs of the indigenous and exotic peoples. It is a form of special interest tourism as different from general tourism which focuses directly on the local people. It involves intimate contact with the "authentic" indigenous culture. In this form of tourism, the tourist visits the homes of the local people and observes and participates in their festivals, and dances. rituals and other forms of cultural expressions. Human contacts with the indigenous people become very important in this form of tourism and it involves a study and purchase of local products as well.

In Ethnic Tourism, however, the emphasis is directly on the traditional cultural forms. The tourists seek to observe or participate in the local festivals and other celebrations. The stress is on the peculiarities of local culture as opposed to the imposing dominance of the homogenizing culture. All this revives the interest of local people in their cultural traditions. This stimulation occurs mainly due to the outsiders' interests in their tradition. Thus, the uniqueness and importance of their folk traditions are brought to the fore and lead to ethnic pride and ethnic solidarity. Ethnic and cultural revitalization is, therefore, a result of this process. This awareness is further developed by a conscious attempt by more advanced members of the local! community to re-educate and re-establish pride in traditional skills and values. There occurs a general revival of interest in traditional festivals and fairs, religious ceremonies, art forms, and craft modulation. Ethnic Tourism also contributes to strengthening ethnic and political identities.

SPIRITUAL TOURISM

Spiritual tourism is about visiting holy and spiritual places of worship belonging to different religions (churches, temples, synagogues, and mosques) and gaining spiritual experience and enlightenment to improve well-being in terms of body, mind, and spirit. Religious tourism, spiritual tourism, sacred tourism, or faith tourism are the names used interchangeably to denote a type of tourism with two main subtypes: pilgrimage, meaning travel for religious or spiritual purposes, and the viewing of religious monuments and artefacts, a branch of sightseeing.

Pilgrimage is spiritually or religiously motivated travel, sometimes over long distances; it has been practised since antiquity and in several of the world's religions. The world's largest mass religious assemblage takes place in India at the Kumbh Mela, which attracts over 120 million pilgrims. Other major pilgrimages include the annual Hajj to Mecca, required once in a Muslim's life.

Religious sightseeing can be motivated by any of several kinds of interest, such as religion, art, architecture, history, and personal ancestry. People can find holy places interesting and moving, whether they are religious or not. Some, such as the churches of Italy, offer fine architecture and major artworks.

GOLF TOURISM

Golf tourism falls under the umbrella of sports tourism, one of the fastest-growing areas in the tourism industry. Although sports tourism is a relatively new concept in contemporary vernacular, its scope of activity is far from a recent phenomenon. The notion of people travelling to participate in and watch sport dates back to the ancient Olympic Games, and the practice of stimulating tourism through sport has existed for over a century.

Golf tourism is an important sector in the tourism industry, in terms of average daily expenditure per visitor. However, golf tourism also generates social and political controversies, mainly due to its impact on the environment.

Golf is currently considered the primary sport in the world in terms of financial expense. Golf and tourism are closely related, so their combination constitutes one of the most critical sectors of the tourism industry. Golf is both a sport and a leisure activity. A Golf tourist is a person who travels and stays away from home to participate in or attend the practice of the sport of golf. Golf tourists established three categories:

(a) tourists whose primary motivation for travel is to play golf;

(b) tourists who play golf as a secondary activity on their vacation or business trips; and

(c) tourists who attend golf tournaments as spectators, or visit golf-related attractions.

SPACE TOURISM

Space tourism is human space travel for recreational purposes. There are several different types of space tourism, including orbital, suborbital, and lunar space tourism. A space tourist was the one who went to space spending his own money and could not be called a professional astronaut, so he was called a "touronaut".

Space tourism is another niche segment of the aviation industry that seeks to give tourists the ability to become astronauts and experience space travel for recreational, leisure, or business purposes. Since space tourism is extremely expensive, it is a case of a very small segment of consumers that are able and willing to purchase a space experience. In April 2001, Dennis Anthony Tito (born August 8, 1940) an American engineer and entrepreneur, became the first space tourist. He funds his trip into space, and he spent nearly eight days in orbit. Tito paid a reported $20 million for his trip. He was sent on a Russian Soyuz spacecraft.

The International Space Station is the most difficult scientific and technological project ever attempted. The International Space Station (ISS) is a modular (habitable artificial satellite) in low Earth orbit (is an Earth-centred orbit close to the planet). it is a multi-nation construction project that is the largest single structure, mankind has ever placed in space. The station's major construction took place between 1998 and 2011, however, it is constantly evolving to include new missions and experiments.

As of 2021, Space Adventures and SpaceX are the only companies to have coordinated tourism flights to Earth's orbit. Virginia-based Space Adventures has worked with Russia to use its Soyuz spacecraft to fly ultra-wealthy individuals to the International Space Station.

PRO-POOR TOURISM

A tourism concept that advocates for tourism as a tool to fight against poverty. It aims at generating net benefits and improving livelihoods. Benefits are not necessarily economic, they might as well be social, cultural, or environmental.Tourism is a means to promote poverty reduction by both international organizations and financially underdeveloped countries because it has the potential to create employment opportunities and foster local economic development.

The past decade has witnessed a remarkable number of studies demonstrating that tourism can assist low-income people with food, housing, medical expenses, and other costs. At the local level, pro-poor tourism can play a significant role in livelihood security and poverty reduction. However, it is often difficult to identify specifically what contributions pro-poor tourism makes, or could make, to accelerate national poverty reduction efforts. There is a growing interest in tourism that aids economic growth via pro-poor tourism in developing countries.

DARK TOURISM

The philosophical investigation of death is the subject of dark tourism. Dark Tourism, also known as Thana tourism, black tourism, morbid tourism, and grief tourism is a type of tourism that involves people taking keen curiosity about visiting places that are historically linked to death and tragedy. Also, places that are reminders of human suffering and bloodshed are subsets of Dark Tourism. Dark places are more appealing because of their historical significance than their connotations with death and pain.

Visitors who are drawn to these areas go so with the objective of better understanding the Other's suffering or just for educational purposes. Dark Tourism imparts both a lesson to future generations as well as enhances the recipient capacity of society through the image of the Other.

Motives for being a Dark Tourist

• Eager to visit the place and feel the ingenuity, after knowing about the destination.

• Self-investigating and obtaining knowledge about such sites to brag about it in social groups

• Fascination, thrill, adventure, and excitement about the destination.

• Self- motives to prove self-maturity or adulthood.

• To pay their tribute, homage, or reflect on the disaster's outcome.

• Aspiration to search for the truth through bizarre investigations

- **Instinct to visit sites with famous memories linked with people or stories of haunted mansions etc**

CHAPTER EIGHT

HEAVENS ON TOURISM

"The most beautiful in the world is, of course, the world itself."

-Wallace Stevens

INCREDIBLE INDIA

India One of the oldest civilizations in the world, India is a mosaic of multicultural experiences. With a rich heritage and myriad attractions, the country is among the most popular tourist destinations in the world. It covers an area of 32, 87,263 sq. km, extending from the snow-covered Himalayan heights to the tropical rain forests of the south. As the 7th largest country in the world, India stands apart from the rest of Asia, marked off as it is by mountains and the sea, which give the country a distinct geographical entity.

1. TAJ MAHAL

The Taj Mahal, often known as the 'Crown of the Palace,' is an ivory-white marble mausoleum on the right bank of the Yamuna River in Agra, India. It was built by the Mughal emperor Shah

Jahan in 1632 to hold the tomb of his favourite wife, Mumtaz Mahal, as well as Shah Jahan's mausoleum. The tomb is placed in formal gardens surrounded on three sides by a crenellated wall and is the centrepiece of a 17-hectare (42-acre) complex that includes a mosque and a guest house. In 1983, the Taj Mahal was named a UNESCO World Heritage Site for being "India's jewel of Muslim art and one of the world's most universally admired masterpieces." The Taj Mahal is a popular tourist destination.

2. KONARK SUN TEMPLE

Konark Sun Temple is a 13th-century CE Sun Temple at Konark on the coastline in Puri district, Odisha, India. Dedicated to the Hindu Sun God Surya, what remains of the temple complex has the appearance of a 100-foot-high chariot with immense wheels and horses, all carved from stone. Once over 200 feet high, much of the temple is now in ruins, in particular, the large shikara tower over the sanctuary; at one time this rose much higher than the mandapa that remains.

The temple that exists today was partially restored by the conservation efforts of British India-era archaeological teams. Declared a UNESCO world heritage site in 1984, it remains a major pilgrimage site for Hindus, who gather here every year for the Chandrabhaga Mela around February. Konark Sun Temple is depicted on the reverse side of the Indian currency note of 10 rupees to signify its importance to Indian cultural heritage.

3. MANALI

Manali is a town in the Indian state of Himachal PradeshA gift of the Himalayas to the world, Manali is a beautiful township nestled in the picturesque Beas River valley. It is known for its cool climate and snow-capped mountains. The tourism industry in Manali started booming only in the early 20th century, The place is a classic blend of peace and tranquillity which makes it a haven for nature lovers and adventure enthusiasts, who want to get off the main tourist trails and experience nature up close. The glacial water of River Beas after rushing down the slopes of Rohtang Pass allows adventure sports activities of rowing white water rafting and river crossing as it meanders through the valley from Manali to Kullu.

4. HAMPI

Hampi or Hampe, also referred to as the Group of Monuments at Hampi, is a UNESCO World Heritage Site located in Hampi town, Vijayanagara district, east-central Karnataka, India. Hampi was the capital of the Vijayanagara Empire in the 14th century. It is a fortified city. Chronicles left by Persian and European travellers, particularly the Portuguese, say that Hampi was a prosperous, wealthy and grand city near the Tungabhadra River, with numerous temples, farms and trading markets. Hampi continues to be an important religious centre, housing the Virupaksha Temple, an active Adi Shankara-linked monastery and various monuments belonging to the old city.

Most of the monuments are Hindu; the temples and the public infrastructure such as tanks and markets include reliefs and artwork depicting Hindu deities and themes from Hindu texts. There are also six Jain temples and monuments and a Muslim mosque and tomb. The architecture is built from the abundant local stone; the dominant style is Dravidian, with roots in the developments in Hindu arts and architecture in the second half of the 1st millennium in the Deccan region.

5. KHAJURAHO

Khajuraho is an ancient city known for magnificent temples and intricate sculptures located in the Chhatarpur district of Madhya Pradesh. Built in the medieval century by the Chandela Dynasty, the UNESCO site of 'Khajuraho Group of Monuments' is famous for its Nagara-Style architecture and graceful sculptures of Manyika and deities.Khajuraho has the country's largest group of medieval Hindu and Jain temples, famous for their erotic sculptures.

The splendour of the intricate statues is one of the reasons that makes it a popular site to visit among tourists. The temples are famous for their craftsmanship that consist of splendid demonstrations of fine sculptures and exceptional architectural skill, making them one of the most stunning UNESCO World Heritage Sites in India. These temples are divided into three groups: Eastern, Western and Southern.

6. ELLORA CAVES

Ellora is a sacred site in Maharashtra, central India. The Ellora Caves are listed by UNESCO as a World Heritage Site and are celebrated for their Hindu, Buddhist, and Jain temples and monuments which were carved from the local cliff rock in the 6th to 8th century CE. Cave 16 features the largest single monolithic rock excavation in the world, the Kailash temple, a chariot-shaped monument dedicated to the god Shiva. The Kailash temple excavation also features sculptures depicting various Hindu deities as well as relief panels summarizing the two major Hindu epics.

There are over 100 caves at the site, all excavated from the basalt cliffs in the Charanandri Hills, 34 of which are open to the public.The Ellora Caves, along with the nearby Ajanta Caves, are a major tourist attraction in the Marathwada region of Maharashtra and a protected monument under the Archaeological Survey of India (ASI).

7. MYSORE PALACE

The Mysore Palace, also known as Amba Vilas Palace, is a historical palace and a royal residence (house). It is located in Mysore, Karnataka. It used to be the official residence of the Wadiyar dynasty and the seat of the Kingdom of Mysore. The palace is in the centre of Mysore and faces the Chamundi Hills eastward. Mysore is commonly described as the 'City of Palaces', and there are seven palaces including this one. However, the Mysore Palace refers specifically to the one within the Old Fort.The architectural style of domes of the palace is commonly described as Indo-Saracenic, with blends of the Hindu, Mughal, Rajput, and Gothic styles.The three-storey stone building of fine grey granite with deep pink marble domes has a facade with several expansive arches and two smaller ones flanking the central arch, which is supported by tall pillars. Apart from its outstanding architecture, the palace is also known for its impeccable roof art, tiles and mosaics, paintings of the royal family, and festive possessions. There also lies display rooms containing old cannons and rifles used by the imperial army, as well as mounted ivory, sandalwood, and pearl boxes, as well as granite carvings of animals.

8. KAZIRANGA NATIONAL PARK

Kaziranga National Park is a national park in the Nagaon district of the state of Assam, India. The sanctuary, which hosts two-thirds of the world's great one-horned rhinoceroses, is a World Heritage Site. Kaziranga is a vast expanse of tall elephant grass, marshland, and dense tropical moist broadleaf forests, crisscrossed by four major rivers, including the Brahmaputra, and the park includes numerous small bodies of water. Kaziranga has been the theme of several books, songs, and documentaries. The park celebrated its centennial in 2005 after its establishment in 1905 as a reserve forest.

9. GOA

The magical land of Goa is a land of celebrations and festivities. Snuggled in the Konkan Coast Belt, It has a long coastline of approx 100 kilometres.The state of Goa, in India, is famous for its beaches and places of worship. Tourism is its primary industry and is generally focused on the coastal areas of Goa, with decreased tourist activity inland. Goa stands out all across the globe for its legacy of the Portuguese colonial regime of more than 450 years and heritage.Major tourist attractions include Bom Jesus Basilica, Fort Aguada, a wax museum on Indian culture, and a heritage museum. The Churches and Convents of Goa have been declared a World Heritage Site by UNESCO.

Beaches are divided into North and South Goa. Goa stands 6th among the top ten Nightlife cities in the world in National

Geographic Travel. A water sport is the prime attraction of the state. Popular beaches such as Baga and Calangute offer jet-skiing, parasailing, banana boat rides, water scooter rides, and much more.

10. DARJEELING

Darjeeling is a city and municipality in the Eastern Himalayas in India, lying at an elevation of 2,100 meters in the state of West Bengal. It is noted for its tea industry, scenic views of the world's third-highest mountain Kangchenjunga, and a narrow-gauge mountain railway, the Darjeeling Himalayan Railway, which is on the UNESCO World Heritage List. The toy train was established back in 1881, the train begins its journey from the plains and rises to over 2000 meters above sea level, offering breathtaking views of the mountains as it chugs along. A large number of inhabitants being Buddhist there are lots of old monasteries present along its length and breadth. Darjeeling is the highest tea exporter and thus, tea tourism in Darjeeling attracts many visitors during the plucking season.

GODS OWN COUNTRY

Kerala, located on the south-western tip of India, enjoys unique geographical features that have made it one of the most sought-after tourist destinations in Asia. Fondly referred to as 'God's Own Country, Kerala was selected by the National Geographic Traveller as one of the 50 destinations of a lifetime and one of the thirteen paradises in the world. An equable climate, serene beaches, tranquil stretches of backwaters, lush hill stations, and exotic wildlife are the major attractions of this land.

Classical art forms, colourful festivals, and exotic cuisine are some of the cultural marvels that await travellers. Ayurveda, the ancient Indian system of medicine, and Panchakarma, the rejuvenation therapy in Ayurveda have also helped Kerala to gain a pan-global reputation as a worth-visit destination. The season never ends in Kerala, because of the year-long moderate climate and numerous festivals and events.

1. WAYANAD

Adorning the northern hills of Kerala is the beautiful district of Wayanad, maintained by the District Tourism Promotion Council, Wayanad. This area is famous for its large amount of camping and trekking trails, breathtaking waterfalls, caves, bird-watching sites, flora, fauna and an overall plethora of magnificent sights.Wayanad's rich history stretches back to the Neolithic Age, with the Edakkal Caves being one of the oldest signs of human settlement to be discovered. The caves seem to have been inhabited by several human settlers over time. Wayanad has a relatively cool climate with a mean temperature of 19 to 32 degrees Celsius.

Kanthanpara Waterfalls is one hotspot in Wayanad that allures tourists from all over the world. Apart from these magnificent falls, Wayanad calls you to experience the stunning beauty of Karapuzha Dam, Pookode & Karlad Lake as well. If you are an adventure seeker, then Cheengari Rock Adventure Center is a must-visit place for you. Another must-visit place in Wayanad is the Edakkal Caves. The caves are two natural rock formations believed to have been formed by a large split in a huge rock. The carvings inside are extremely beautiful.

2. MUNNAR

Munnar "Kashmir of South India" is a popular honeymoon destination, is a town and hill station in the Idukki district of the southwestern Indian state of Kerala. Munnar rises as three mountain streams merge - Mudrapuzha, Nallathanni and Kundala. 1,600 m above sea level, this hill station was once the summer resort of the erstwhile British Government in South India. Sprawling tea plantations, picturesque towns, winding lanes and holiday facilities make this a popular resort town. Among the exotic flora found in the forests and grasslands here is the Neelakurinji. This flower which bathes the hills in blue once every twelve years will bloom next in 2030. Munnar also has the highest peak in South India, Anamudi, which towers over 2,695 m. Munnar is noted for several threatened and endemic species including Nilgiri Thar, the grizzled giant squirrel, the Nilgiri wood-pigeon, elephant, the gaur, and the Nilgiri langur, and the sambar.

3. VEMBANAD LAKE

Vembanad, also known as Punnamada, is India's longest and largest lake, as well as the largest in Kerala. It is known as Vembanadu Lake in Kottayam, Vaikom, Changanassery, Punnamada Lake in Alappuzha, Punnappra, Kuttanadu, and Kochi Lake in Kochi. The Kochi Lake region contains several small islands, including Vypin, Mulavukad, Maradu, Udayamperoor, Vallarpadam, and Willingdon Island. Kochi Port is developed around the islands of Willingdon and Vallarpadam.

Kuttanad, also known as The Rice Bowl of Kerala, has the lowest altitude in India and is also one of the few places in the world where cultivation takes place below sea level. Kuttanad lies on the southern portion of Vembanad.

The Nehru Trophy Boat Race is conducted in a portion of the lake.Vembanad Lake is at the heart of Kerala Backwaters tourism with hundreds of kettuvallams plied on it and numerous resorts on its banks. The Kumarakom Bird Sanctuary is located on the east coast of the lake. The lake has become a major tourist attraction. High levels of pollution have been noticed at certain hotspots of the Vembanad backwaters.

4. KOVALAM

Kovalam is a region in the city of Trivandrum,Kovalam is an internationally renowned beach with three adjacent crescent beaches. It has been a favourite haunt of tourists since the 1930s. A massive rocky promontory on the beach has created a beautiful bay of calm waters ideal for sea bathing.

The leisure options at this beach are plenty diverse. Sunbathing, swimming, herbal body toning massages, special cultural programmes and catamaran cruising are some of them. The tropical sun acts so fast that one can see the faint blush of coppery tan on the skin in a matter of minutes. Life on the beach begins late in the day and carries on well into the night. The beach complex includes a string of budget cottages, Ayurvedic health resorts, convention facilities, shopping zones, swimming pools, and Yoga and Ayurvedic massage centres.

5. Athirappilly Waterfalls

Athirappilly Falls, "The Niagara of South India" the largest waterfall in Kerala is situated in Chalakudy Taluk of Thrissur District in Kerala, on the Chalakudy River, which originates from the upper reaches of the Western Ghats at the entrance to the Sholayar ranges. Barely 5 km away is another family favourite, Vazhachal Waterfalls. These waterfalls became famous for not just their view but the endemic species found in the surrounding dense forests. Researchers have found four endangered species of the Hornbill here, the only place they thrive in the entire Western Ghats. Ornithologists attach great significance to this location and bird watchers can come across many rare and vibrant species in these parts.

The journey from Chalakkudy to Athirappilly Falls passes through a landscape of winding roads, small villages, and lush green trees. Visitors can reach the top of the waterfall via a paved path that leads through thick bamboo clusters. From Angamaly, the route is in the midst of an Oil Palm Reserve at Ezhattumugham tourism village. A steep narrow path or a wide staired path can be taken to the bottom of the falls.

6. BEKAL FORT

Bekal Fort is a medieval fort located in North Malabar, Kasargod District built by Shivappa Nayaka of Keladi in 1650 AD, at Bekal. It is the largest fort in Kerala, spreading over 40 acres. Bekal Fort was not an administrative centre and does not include any palaces or mansions. . This historic monument offers a superb view of the Arabian Sea from its tall observation towers, which were occupied by gigantic cannons till a few centuries ago. Near the Fort is an old Mosque that is said to have been built by Tipu Sultan of Mysore.

The fort's zigzag entrance and surrounding trenches reveal its defensive strategy. Holes on the outer walls are designed to defend the fort effectively from naval attacks. The upper holes are meant for aiming at the farthest targets; the lower holes below for striking as enemy nearer and the lowest holes to attack the enemy closest to the fort. India declared Bekal Fort a special tourism area in 1992 and formed Bekal Tourism Development Corporation three years later to promote it.

7. FORT KOCHI

Fort Kochi, the western part of the Kochi city of Ernakulam district in Kerala. It is about 12 km away from Ernakulam Town. Fort Kochi has played an important role in the history of Kerala. Fort Kochi also has several attractions like the Santa Cruz Basilica. Fort Kochi also houses many historical monuments such as the St. Francis Church, the first church of Vasco da Gama, the Dutch Seminary, the China Vela and many others. The Indian Navy's ship, Dronacharya, is located in Fort Kochi.

The Mattancherry Palace is close by. Fort Kochi was the first European township in Kerala. The Fort Kochi carnival celebrates New Year's Eve every year. Thousands of people come to visit this carnival. The car rides and other festive events are also part of the carnival.

8. PADMANABHASWAMY TEMPLE

Located inside the East Fort in Thiruvananthapuram, the capital city of the State of Kerala in India is the Sree Padmanabha Swamy Temple dedicated to Lord Vishnu. This temple is a blend of the Kerala and Dravidian styles of architecture. It is believed to be the world's richest temple.The presiding deity of this temple is Lord Vishnu, reclining on Anantha, the hooded Serpent. The shrine is currently run by a trust headed by the erstwhile royal family of Travancore.

The temple also has some interesting structural features in the form of Bali Peeda Mandapam and Mukha Mandapam. These are halls, decorated with beautiful sculptures of various Hindu deities. Another structure that captures attention here is the Navagraha Mandapa the ceiling of which displays the navagrahas (the nine planets).

9. MALAMPUZHA GARDEN AND DAM

Malampuzha Garden in Palakkad district is the only rock-cut garden in South India made by Nek Chand, the renowned artist and winner of the prestigious Padmashree Award. The entire garden is made from broken pieces of bangles, tiles, used plastic cans, tins and other waste materials. Also situated in the gardens is the massive Malampuzha Yakshi (female vampire) built in 1969 by Kanayi Kunhiraman, a greatly respected sculptor from the state. It is a spectacular relic of art that we are lucky to still have with us. The flowering beds, fountains and rose gardens along with an aerial ropeway make it a place that instantly soothes your soul.

In the lower hills of the Western Ghats lies the beautiful Malampuzha township whose lush greenery and a plethora of picnic spots make it a must-visit spot in these areas. It has really good trekking trails that are available to all with a penchant for the same. Malampuzha Gardens and the Irrigation Dam tend to be the areas that attract the highest number of visitors.

10. KOZHIKODE

Kozhikode s a city along the Malabar Coast in the state of Kerala in India. Kozhikode was once the most prominent region of the Malabar coast that witnessed the arrival of Arab, Chinese and East African traders. Vasco da Gama landed on its shores in 1498, shooting the region to global fame. Kozhikode played a major role in the trade and commerce of ancient Kerala by being the capital of the influential Zamorin.

The central Kozhikode Beach, overlooked by an old lighthouse, is a popular spot for watching the sunset, Inland, tree-lined Mananchira Square, with its musical fountain, surrounds the massive Mananchira Tank, an artificial pond, Lush green countryside, serene beaches, historic sites, wildlife sanctuaries, rivers and hills make Kozhikode a popular destination.The village of Kallayi is situated on the banks of the river Kallayi. It has an archaic charm and was a busy timber trade centre during the late nineteenth and early twentieth centuries.

CHAPTER NINE

HEADS IN BEDS

"Education is the most powerful weapon which you can use to change the world" --Nelson Mandela

ACCOMMODATION INDUSTRY

Accommodation is one of the most crucial aspects of a destination. Any traveller choosing to visit any destination would firstly look for accommodation suited to his/her needs. It should provide him/her food and beverage services, resting facilities, etc. up to his satisfaction level. Accommodation units themselves act as tourist attractions for a large number of people.Accommodation includes food and lodging facilities for different types of guests. Accommodation should be comfortable and Good quality of services & facilities should be provided to the guest by the accommodation unit.

According to the World Tourism Organisation, WTO Report on The Development of the Accommodation Sector, tourist accommodation is used to denote the facilities operated for short accommodation of guests, either with or without service, against payment and according to fixed rates. For term classification, all tourist accommodation has been divided into the following groups:

(i) hotels and similar establishments (the hotel industry proper) and,

(ii) supplementary means of accommodation.

EARLY HISTORY

The early history of accommodation for travellers can be said to have its origin in the Greek Word 'Xenia'. By this word, ancient Greeks meant not only hospitality but also all forms of protection given to a visiting stranger.

Travelling during this period was not an easy affair. Travellers were mainly diplomats, philosophers, intellectuals and researchers. There were no lodgings specially designed to receive visitors. Guests were invited to stay in the dwellings of noblemen. This was rather a gift comprising a place to stay, food, care and a bath.

As travelling became more frequent, accommodation for travellers was viewed in two ways. The institution of 'inns' came into being. Inns can perhaps be considered to be the first such accommodation units which catered to the needs of travellers in early times. During the Roman Empire, many such inns were established that provided food, drink and also entertainment to weary travellers.

After the advent of Christianity, it was the Church which came to the rescue of the travellers. Travel grew again for religious pilgrimage purposes. By the 15th century, the institution of the inn once again developed in several countries in Europe, especially in England and France.

In the United States of America another type of accommodation unit, known as the 'tavern, was opened in the year 1634 by a man called Samuel Coles, taverns were popular meeting places where people used to come for eating, drinking and entertainment.

The institution of the hotel had its beginning in the early fourteenth century. The first hotel in the classical sense, the forerunner of the present-day existing complex unit, is said to have been created in Paris, in the year 1312. The next fifty years saw a gradual increase in the hotels and resorts in many countries of Europe. By the year 1820, 'hotel' became the accepted term to describe a place where people stayed for the night and took their meals on payment. In the 1820s the first tourist hotel appeared in Switzerland.

In India, the concept of shelter for travellers is not new. It's as old as its recorded history. The historical records are replete with the mention/references of viharas, Dharamsala, saris, musafirkhanas, etc. These establishments provided a home to all wayfarers, be they pilgrims, scholars, adventurers or merchants. The shelter under various names has always been a part of India's culture as a valuable institution, providing a vital service. The ancient Buddhist monks were probably the first to institutionalise the concept of shelter in India.

TYPES OF ACCOMMODATION

According to the organisation for Economic Cooperation and categories Development (OECD) accommodations are classified into two "hotels and similar establishments and "Supplementary means of accommodation". Following are the main categories of hotels.

Hotels

A hotel is defined by British Law as a 'place where bonafide travellers can receive food or shelter, provided he or she is in a position to pay for it and is in a fit condition to be received.

1. International Hotel

International hotels are the modern western-style hotels located in almost all metropolitan and other large cities as well as principal tourist centres. These hotels are luxury hotels and reclassified based on an internationally accepted system of classification. These hotels provide, in addition to accommodation, all the other facilities which make the stay a very comfortable and interesting experience. These facilities include well-appointed reception and information counter, banquet halls, conference facilities, deposit facilities, multi-cuisine restaurants, in-house shopping, entertainment etc.

2. RESORT HOTELS

Resort hotels cater to the needs of the holiday-maker, the tourist and those, who for reasons of health, desire a change of atmosphere. Resort hotels are located near the sea, mountains and other areas abounding in natural beauty. Rest, relaxation and entertainment are the key factors around which resorts are built. The primary motive of a person visiting them is rest which he is looking for, away from his routine, busy work life.

3. Commercial Hotels

Commercial hotels direct their appeal primarily to the individual traveller as compared to international or resort hotels where the focus is on group travel. Most commercial hotels receive guests who are on business although some have permanent guests. As the hotel caters primarily to people who are visiting a place for commerce or business, these are located in important commercial and industrial centres of large towns and cities.

4. Residential Hotel Resort Hotels

These hotels can be described as apartment houses complete with hotel services. These are often referred to as apartment hotels. The tariff of rooms in these hotels is charged on a monthly, half-yearly or yearly basis and is charged for either furnished or unfurnished accommodation. These hotels, which are located mostly in big cities, operate exclusively under the European plan where no meals are provided to the guests.

5. Floating Hotels

As the name suggests, these hotels are located on the surface of the water. It may be on the sea or a lake. All the facilities and services of a hotel are provided here and these are very popular in many countries. In some countries, old luxury ships have been converted into floating hotels and are very popular among tourists.

6. Capsule Hotels

The capsule is a box made of glass-reinforced plastic or cement, concentrated some -bed, a clock, radio, open either at one side or one end, in which are of the functions of a traditional hotel room are lined up in double TV, flexible lighting, a box for valuables and a miniature table for writing. Rooms in a capsule hotel generally decker fashion along a central aisle as in a sleeping compartment of a train. Toilets and washrooms, vending machine room, and lounge are close by on each floor, of the hotel. The functions of each capsule are controlled and monitored by a central computer system and the security is controlled by closed-circuit TV cameras. The hotels cater mainly to business travellers.

7. Airport Hotels

Airport hotels, as the name suggests, are located near the airports to offer comfort and primarily to cater to the needs of transit passengers, airports c also passengers of delayed or cancelled flights. The various facilities crew as a convenience to the air travellers. The various services that may include provided in these hotels are designed Parking and shuttle services to and from the airport terminal.

SUPPLEMENTARY ACCOMMODATION

All establishments under the heading of supplementary accommodation are designed to offer the possibility of staying overnight and having meals in return for cash payment per day and based on services provided. The standard of comfort is modest compared to that of a hotel. On the other hand, however, there are certain inherent advantages to this type of accommodation. The biggest advantage is that of price. It is moderately priced. In addition, the atmosphere is informal and there is more freedom about the dress, etc. There is also more emphasis on entertainment and sports resulting in increased social contact among the guests.

The following are some of the principal forms of supplemental accommodation:

(i) Motel

The motel was meant for local motorists and foreign tourists travelling by road. Primarily designed to serve the needs of motorists, motels almost exclusively meet the demand for transit accommodation. They serve the function of a transit hotel except that they are geared to accommodate motor travelling guests for overnight stays. The important services provided by motels include parking, garage facilities, accommodation, restaurant facilities, public catering and recreational facilities.

(ii) Youth Hostel

A Youth hostel can be defined as a building which offers clean, moderate and inexpensive shelter to young people exploring their own country or other countries and travelling independently or in groups on holiday or for educational purposes. It is a place where young people of different social backgrounds and nationalities meet and come to know each other. The objective of youth hostels, therefore, is not merely to provide accommodation and board, but also to serve as centres which offer an opportunity to young people coming from different parts of the country, as also young travellers from abroad, to know and understand each other.

(iii) Caravan and Camping Sites

These are also known as open-air hostels, tourist camps or camping grounds. Camping, originally practised by hikers on foot, is increasingly giving way to car camping. The sites are usually located within large cities in open spaces. Equipped to receive mobile accommodation in the form of caravans, the camping sites provide facilities for parking, tent pitching, water, electricity, toilet, etc. Though the services provided generally include restaurants, recreational rooms, toilets and at certain places, a grocer's shop, the type of services often varies from place to place.

(iv) Pension

Pension is also described as a private hotel, a guest house or a is made in advance. Mostly managed by a family, a pension is much cheaper than a hotel. Catering facilities are optional and are usually restricted to the residents. Many of them stay for longer and definite periods such as a week or a fortnight.

(v) Bed and Breakfast Establishments

Also known in some countries as apartment hotels and hotel grains, they represent a growing form of accommodation units catering fa or holiday as well as business travellers. These establishments provide only accommodation and breakfast but not the principal meals. These are usually located in large towns and cities, along commercial and holiday routes.

CATEGORIZATION IN INDIA

Classification based on Star.

The classification is done by the Ministry of Tourism under which a committee forms known as HRACC (Hotels and Restaurants Approval & Classification Committee) headed by the Director-General of tourism with a panel consisting of experts from the industry. This is a permanent committee to classify hotels into 1–5-star categories. Generally, inspects once in three years.

1 Star

- These are smaller hotels managed by proprietors. The hotel often has a more personal atmosphere. The hotel should have at least 10 lettable bedrooms.
- 25% should have an attached bathroom with a bathroom for every four of the remaining room.
- 25% of the bathroom should have western-style WCs
- Reception counter with a telephone and a telephone for the use of guests.
- It is usually located near an affordable attraction, major intersections and convenient transportation.
- Furnishings and facilities are clean but basic. Most will not have a restaurant on site but are usually within walking distance.

2 Star

- The building should be constructed and the locality and environs including the approach suitable for a good hotel.
- There should be a reception counter with a telephone.
- All public and private rooms should be fully air-conditioned and should be well equipped with the support quality
- There should be experienced, courteous and efficient staff in smart and clean uniforms
- Should have at least 10 lettable rooms with at least75% should attached bathrooms with showers.
- At least 25 % of the rooms should be air-conditioned.
- Telephone in each room and telephone for the use of guests and visitors and provision for radio or relayed music in each room.
- carpets, curtains, carpets, luxury furniture of high standards fittings etc.

3 Star

Typically, these hotels offer spacious accommodation that includes well-appointed staff and decorated lobbies.

- Should have at least 20 lettable rooms with attached bathrooms with long baths or most modern shower chamber.
- At least 50 % of the rooms should be air-conditioned and the furniture and furnishings such as carpets, curtains etc. should be a very good standard.
- There should be a receptionist, cash and information counter attended by the highest qualified trained and experienced personnel and conference facilities.
- There should be provision for reliable laundry and dry cleaning services.24 hrs housekeeping at the hotel should be

of the highest possible standard and there should be a plentiful supply of linen, blankets etc which should be of the highest quality available.

- Telephone in each room. and telephone for the use of guests and visitors and provision for radio or relayed music in each room.
- Bell desk services are generally not available. They are located near the business area for immediate approach and the environs should be of the highest standard.
- There should be well equipped, well-furnished and well-maintained dining room/restaurant on the premises.

4 Star

Architectural features and general construction of the hotel building should have distinctive qualities.

- Should have at least 25 lettable rooms with attached bathrooms with long baths or most modern shower chamber.
- At least 50 % of the bathroom must have long baths or the most modern shower chambers with 24 hrs service of hot and cold running water.
- There should be a special restaurant dining room where facilities for dancing are also available.
- Telephone in each room. and telephone for the use of guests and visitors and provision for radio or relayed music in each room.
- The locality including the immediate approach and environs should be of the highest standard.
- There should be a receptionist, cash and information counter attended by the highest qualified trained and experienced personnel and conference facilities.

5 Star

Architectural features and general construction of the hotel building should have distinctive qualities.

- Should have at least 25 lettable rooms with attached bathrooms with long baths or most modern shower chamber.
- At least 50 % of the bathroom must have long baths or the most modern shower chambers with 24 hrs service of hot and cold running water.
- There should be provision for reliable laundry and dry-cleaning services.24 hrs housekeeping at the hotel should be of the highest possible standard and there should be a plentiful supply of linen, blankets etc which should be of the highest quality available.
- The locality including the immediate approach and environs should be of the highest standard.
- There should be a receptionist, cash and information counter attended by the highest qualified trained and experienced personnel and conference facilities.
- Adequate parking space and swimming pool.
- Offer both international and Indian cuisine and the food &beverage services should be of the highest standards
- 24 hrs services for reception information and telephone.

DEPARTMENT IN HOTEL

A hotel can provide good service, when its all department will work together efficiently and effectively, by showing good team wteamworkdination and communication. The most important function of a hotel is to provide Food and shelter to prospective guests. To provide food & shelter, there is several departments or Ares, who all function together round-the-clock inside hotel premises.

All departments are broadly categorized in two parts:

1. OPERATIONAL DEPARTMENT (CORE DEPARTMENT):

· Front office
· Food & Beverage service
· Housekeeping
· Food production (kitchen)

2. ADMINISTRATIVE DEPARTMENT (NON-CORE DEPARTMENT)

· Maintenance department
· Account department
· Human resource department
· Electronic data processing department
· Communication department
· Security department
· Purchase department
· Stores
· Sales & marketing department

Each department is equally important for the proper functioning of the hotel. Each department are been explained as follows:

A. FRONT OFFICE

The main function of the department is:

- To allot the room to the guest, called as check-in.
- To maintain the room records for reservation and allocation.
- To collect the room charges and other miscellaneous charges for various services used by a guest during his/her stay at the hotel, at the time of departure of the guest.

- To make a booking for rooms.
- To handle the phone calls of the hotel.

Different sections of the Front office:

Front Desk

- Reception: this section is used for the check-in process of the guest.
- Information: this section is used for providing various information to in-house guests.
- Cashier desk: this section is used for the checkout process of the guest.
- Guest relation desk: this section is used for collecting guest feedback and maintenance of guest history.
- Bell desk: this section is used for the assistanceguestsuest during the check-in and checkout process.
- Travel desk: this section is used for the stance of guests for arranging vehicles for guest movements and for making train/aeroplane reservations.

Back Office

- Reservation desk: this section is used for taking booking rooms.
- Telephone operator: this section is used for attending to all phone calls land up in the hotel or for providing a trunk dial facility to guests.
- Business centcentreis section is used for secrthe etarial job of the guest.

B. HOUSEKEEPING DEPARTMENT

The main function of this department is:

- To take care of the cleanliness of rooms, the hotel building and its furniture and furnishings.
- To maintain the linen room for maintenance of room linen, restaurant linen etc.
- To maintain the gardening work of the hotel.
- To maintain a guest laundry facility for room guests.
- To maintain a staff laundry facility for staff of a hotel.

Different sections of the department:

- Linen room
- Housekeeping desk
- Housekeeping store
- In-House laundry
- Gardening department

C. Food & Beverage service department

The main function of this department is

- To provide food & beverage facilities to the guest.
- To provide food & beverage for groups, conferences, meetings, theme parties etc.

The different sections are:

- Restaurant
- Room Service department
- Banquet department
- Bar & lounge

D. Food Production (Kitchen):

The main function of this department is:

- To provide various types of dishes to the guest as per the menu.
- To provide food for various buffet or banquet parties.
- To provide food to the staff of a hotel.
- To prepare different types of dishes for a special occasion.

Different sections of the kitchen:

- Hot Kitchen: North Indian
- South Indian
- Tandoor section
- Chinese or oriental kitchen
- Halwai or Indian sweet section
- Pantry or salad section: tea/coffee, juices, salads, breakfast items etc.
- Butchery or cold kitchen: for making different types of chicken, mutton, beef cuts etc.
- Bakery and confectionary: for making cookies, cakes, pastries etc.

MAINTENANCE DEPARTMENT

The main functions of this department are:

- To maintain all the equipment s placed inside or related to the hotel.
- To be responsible for smooth supply of electricity, water, and smooth function of air conditioning unit.
- To be responsible for AMC of important and expensive equipment
- To maintain all the furniture and fixtures of rooms and other areas of the hotel.

ACCOUNT DEPARTMENT

The main function of this department is:

- Preparation of budget and allocation of revenue and expenditure for various department
- Maintain all account-related books by the government rules and regulations.
- Preparation of the balance sheet of the company.
- Liaising with Govt. offices for tax and revenue-related matters.
- Collection of revenue from guests, companies etc.
- Giving salaries to employees.
- To keep a check on the food & beverage cost.
- To keep a check on the purchase and sale of alcoholic beverages for the property.
- To keep the account of revenue generated and expenditure under various heads for each department.

HUMAN RESOURCE DEPARTMENT

The main function of this department is:

- Recruitment and selection of employees for the hotel as per requirement.
- Training and development of employee
- Maintenance of attendance records, leave records etc.
- Maintenance of personal file for each employee with all details, for periodically periodical

ELECTRONIC DATA PROCESSING DEPARTMENT

The main function of this department is:

- Maintenance of the Property management system of the hotel
- Maintenance of various aspects of the Internet and its related matters.
- Generatioof n various relevant electronic data as per requirements t of the hotel.
- Maintenance of all computer units hired or purchased by the hotel. And its relevant software.

COMMUNICATION DEPARTMENT

The main function of this department is:

- Maintenance of telephone connections for each room in another breathe ea of the hotel.
- Maintenance of cable connections of televisions in rooms and other places of the hotel.
- Maintenance of audio-visual equipment for conferences and parties.
- Maintenance of audio-visual equipment of the hotel.

SECURITY DEPARTMENT

The main function of this department is:

- To be responsible fothforsafetyy and security of guests of hotel tel.
- To be responsible for the safety o employees.
- To keep a check on theft cases of the hotel.
- To cooperate with staff on fire exit procedures.
- To keep records of received materials and dispatched materials of or for the property.
- To keep a record of the f movement of fixeassetshe ts of property.
- To keep a check on unauthorized entry of people.

PURCHASE DEPARTMENT & STORES

The main function of this department is:

- To purchase materials from the market athe the requirements of various departments of the hotel.
- To purchase all tequipmentuipments and materials for the hotel the l.
- To liaison with different compvendorsor vendors for supply of perishable or non-perishable goods.
- To liaison with different dethe alertfanonovegetarian nononongetarian items (chicken, mutton, fish, beef, etc.)
- To store all the purchased items properlyruleser basic rule.
- To issue the material to the user department of the hotel after making g prorecordscord.
- To maintain the smooth flow of perishable and non-perishable goods for the department.

SALES & MARKETING DEPARTMENT

The main function of this department is:

- To sell the room nights and varconferenceences facilities to various clientele.
- To sell the room nights to individguestsuest for holpurposesrpose.
- To make the brand image of catheterseter in the market.
- To act as an agent for the hotel and provide variousinformationnonf changes and updating.

TYPES OF ROOMS

- ### *SINGLE ROOM*

The room has one single bed, meant for one person.

- ### *TWIN ROOM*

The room has two single beds, separated from each other by a bedside table, meant for two people.

- ### *DOUBLE ROOM*

The room has one composite double bed, meant for two people.

- *SUITE*

A suite comprises foremen in one room. It is an apartment having one bedroom with one composite double bed & a parlparloure décor of such unit is of very high standards, very expensive Normally suite has a theme, & is named after this timepiece

- *CABANA*

Rooms situated away from main hukihikingar swimming pool or sen beach, used for changing & resting purpose.

- *LANAI*

Rooms with a good view, normally over viewing hills, garden, mountains.

- *STUDIO ROOM*

Room with one single bed and sofas which can be converted to a bed (sofa cum bed).

- *HOLLYWOOD TWIN BEDDED ROOM*

Type of twin room with coma mon head headboard

- *MURPHY BEDDED ROOM:*

Room with a bed which can be folded against the wall, provide large floor area.

- *INTERCONNECTING ROOM*

Two rooms have a common wall and a door that connects the two rooms. This allows guests to access any of the two rooms without passing through the corridor.

- *DUPLEX*

Rooms have two levels under one roothe, f, the uplevel level bedroom and andthetand the lower level is used for the living room, connected by an internal staircase. Rooms are expensive, generally used by the business client who wishes to use the lower poofficen licensee ficece and upper-level aa s bedroom.

- *JUNIOR SUITE*

Large room converted to a suite by a partition. Not very expensive but priced highly ta han regular room.

-

PENTHOUSE SUITE

Situated at terrace level or top most floor of hotels and has an attached open terrace or open sky space. It has exclusive décor and furnishing and is among the costliest rooms of the hotel.

- *QUAD*

Room with four beds to provide sleeping accommodation to four people.

- *TRIPLE ROOM*

A room has three beds, three pax can stay in the room;

- *DOUBLE DOUTheThe room*

The room has two double beds and can accommodate four people.

- *SPATT ROOM*

special attention a room, room meant for the physically challenged guest

-

SINGLE LADY ROOM

rooms specially designed for the ladies travelling alone. These rooms are designed keeping in mind the needs of the lady guests.

TYPES OF HOTEL MEAL PLANS

I. American Meal Plan

Room Rent+ Buffet Breakfast+ Buffet Lunch+ Buffet Dinner

II. Modified American Plan

Room Rent+ Buffet Breakfast+ (Buffet Lunch/Buffet Dinner)

III. Continental Plan

Room Rent+ Buffet Breakfast only

IV. European Plan

Room Rent only

CHAPTER TEN

THE BUSSINES OF TRAVEL

"One's destination is never a place, but a new way of seeing things."

~~Henry Miller

TRAVEL AGENCY

"A travel agency is a private retailer or public service that offers several types of travel packages for each destination on behalf of hotel or travel suppliers. Outdoor recreation activities, airlines, car rentals, cruise lines, hotels, railways, travel insurance, package tours, insurance, guide books, VIP airport lounge access, arranging logistics for luggage and medical items delivery for travellers on request, public transportation schedules, car rentals, and bureau de change services are all services that travel agencies can provide. Airlines that do not have operations in a specific location can use travel companies as broad sales agents."

A travel agency's main function is to act as an agent, selling travel products and services on behalf of a supplier. Travel agencies are frequently compensated by providers with commissions and other bonuses and incentives, or they may charge a fee to end-users. Travel agencies often receive a greater commission from hotel owners and tour operators, whereas airlines receive a lower commission.

TYPES

Travel agencies are categorized into two types-: Retail Travel Agency and Wholesale Travel Agency

1. RETAIL TRAVEL AGENCY

According to SARC (1967), " retail travel agency business consists of the activities involved in selling tourism products/ services directly to the tourists and performs normal functions such as issuing air tickets, making accommodation and transportation reservation, providing specialized services, and accepting and making payments".

A retail travel agency operates similarly to any other store, selling tourist products directly to visitors on behalf of the supplier and earning a commission. Its primary source of revenue is commission. A two-way selling approach based on commission and mark-up price is also used. A marked-up price refers to the marking-up of the cost of the tour and selling it at a higher price. The difference between retail price and wholesale cost is known as mark-up price.

2. WHOLESALE TRAVEL AGENCY

These agencies are specialized in organizing package tours, which are marketed to the customers/tourists through the network of a retail travel agency or directly to the prospective clients if the wholesale travel agency has a retail division. A wholesale travel agency purchases tourists' product components in bulk and designs tour packages.

A wholesale travel agency may purchase travel components in bulk from a provider and resell them to other travel businesses. Wholesale travel agencies put together vacation packages that retail travel agencies sell to customers. A typical package tour comprises air tickets, lodging, and sometimes extra services such as entertainment, sightseeing, and sports activities, among others. The majority of these cruises include the services of escorts, however, a handful is sold to customers who want to go solo.

FUNCTIONS

The functions performed by a travel agency depend upon the scope of activities size and location. The following are the major functions performed by the travel agency-

1. Provision of Travel Information

Information is the first and foremost function of a travel agency. This is a very specialized job and the person behind the counter should be a specialist. A good travel agent is something of a personal counsellor who knows all the details about the travel and also the needs and interests of the intending traveller.

2. Liaison with Providers of Services

In the travel trade, there are a lot of intermediaries are involved, before any form of travel can be sold over the counter, contracts have to be entered into with the principal providers of various services. These include transportation companies, hotel proprietors, surface transport like motorcars or coaches for transfers to and from hotels and sightseeing, etc.

3. Identification of profile of target market

The travel agency has to select a particular market segment it wants to cater to because possibly one cannot serve all kinds of clients effectively. Once a particular market segment or more than one segment is selected, he has to prepare their profile i.e. what age, sex, income, education, and social groups they belong to because ultimately there, preference for destination, transport and accommodation and purchasing power depends upon these factors.

4. Preparation of tour Itineraries

A tourist itinerary is a composition of a series of operations that are a result of the study of the market. A tourist journey is characterised by an itinerary using various means of transport to link one locality with another. The preparation of different types of itineraries is another important function of a travel agency. The development and implementation of itineraries necessitate flawless technological and administrative organisation, as well as awareness of public holiday desires.

5. Ticketing

Another significant duty of a travel agency is to sell tickets to clients for various modes of transportation such as air, rail, and sea. Due to frequent changes in international and domestic airline schedules, as well as the arrival of new flights, the job of the travel agent has been more difficult in recent years. A computerised reservation system (CRS) has rather revolutionised the reservation system both for air and rail seats and also a room in a hotel.

6. Documentation and foreign exchange procedures

If the travel includes an international journey, the travel agent is responsible to make necessary arrangements for travel documents, which are needed to enter a foreign country like passport, visa, health documents etc... No trade can take place without the presence of forex, the conversion of one country's currency into another. Approved travel agency authorized by Govt. body provides currency exchange services to tourists.

7. Reservation and Booking

It is a very important function of all types of travel agencies. A travel agency consistently makes linkage with the accommodation sector, transport sector and other entertainment organizations to reserve rooms, and seats in the cultural programs and transportation.

8. Travel Insurance

It is a very important function of all types of travel agencies. A travel agency consistently makes linkage with the accommodation sector, transport sector and other entertainment organizations to reserve rooms, and seats in the cultural programs and transportation.

9. Preparation, costing and marketing of tour package

Travel agencies prepare and market tour packages and sell them to tourists. The coasting and pricing of tour packages depend to a large extent on the ability of travel agents to how effectively he can negotiate with the principal suppliers.

10. Meeting and Incentive Planning

The business events sector is one of the highest-yielding inbound tourism segments. Meeting and incentive planners organise and manage all aspects of meetings and events including conventions, conferences, incentives, seminars, workshops, symposiums, exhibitions and special events. Meeting and incentive planners use a wide variety of venues, tour operators, accommodation, team building companies and restaurants.

TOUR OPERATOR

A tour operator is a business that typically combines and organizes accommodations, meals, sightseeing and transportation components, to create a package tour. They advertise and produce brochures to promote their products, holidays and itineraries. Tour operators can sell directly to the public or sell through travel agents or a combination of both.

Today, tour operators have become highly competitive. They endeavour to achieve a high volume of turnover and maximum International and domestic market share by effectively operating. Moreover, the success of many developed and developing nations as tourist destinations depend heavily on a tour operator's ability to attract tourists, development and promotion of tourism plant, diversification of tourism product and their social responsibilities to develop the remote and backward area.

TYPES OF TOUR OPERATORS

Tour operators come in all shapes and sizes. Some are large, multinational organisations and others are small, independent businesses. Different types of tour operators develop products for different types of tourism. This can include the mass market, niche tourism market, special interest tourism, the luxury market, tailor-made products and dynamic packages.

Tour operators are categorized into four types. These are categories based on the nature of the business and its operations.

1. Inbound Tour Operators
2. Outbound Tour Operators

3. Domestic Tour Operators
4. Ground Operators

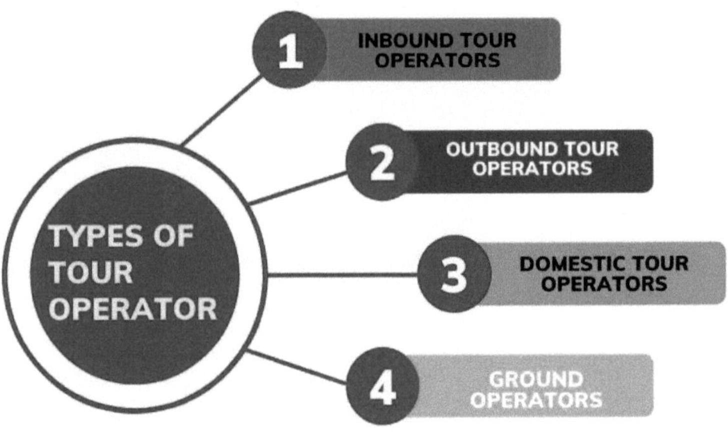

1. Inbound tour operators

An inbound tour operator facilitates inbound tourism. An inbound tour operator aims to bring tourists into a particular country or country. Inbound tour operators will often collaborate with local travel agencies and transport operators to facilitate travel arrangements for their customers.

For example, a group of American Tourists is coming through TCI Ltd. to India and the company makes arrangements and handles the group in India then TCI is called an inbound tour operator.

2. Outbound tour operators

An outbound tour operator facilitates outbound tourism. An outbound tour operator aims to send tourists out of a particular country or country. Outbound tour operators will often collaborate with foreign travel agencies and transport operators to facilitate travel arrangements for their customers.

For example, a group of American tourists going on a trip to India and Thomas Cook handle arrangements in America like ticket reservation, hotel booking etc. then Thomas Cook is called Outbound Tour operators in the context of America.

3. Domestic tour operators

A domestic tour operator facilitates domestic tourism. A domestic tour operator aims to organise travel within a particular country or country. Domestic tour operators will often collaborate with domestic travel agencies and transport operators to facilitate travel arrangements for their customers. Domestic tour operators will often also serve the inbound tourism market.

4. Ground tour operators

These are commonly known as handling agencies and their main function is to organize tour arrangements for incoming tourists on behalf of overseas operators. When a tour operator himself promotes beach holidays, wildlife holidays, adventure and heritage tours, and cultural tours at different places then the role of the ground operator becomes effective. It is the ground operator who by handling the incoming travellers at different places makes the tour successful.

FUNCTIONS

1. Planning a Tour

The tour operator's most significant role is to plan a tour. Trip operators arrange a tour and create a tour itinerary that includes the origin, destination, and all points of interest in a traveller's journey. A potential tour operator can also advise incoming travellers on the many types of tour programmes available for their leisure or business travel.

2. Making Tour Package

Individual travel components are purchased individually from providers by tour operators and then combined into a package tour. Tour operators assemble numerous travel components into a finished product called a tour package, which is then sold to tourists at their pricing. Tour Operators are also responsible for creating tour packages.

3. Arranging a Tour

Tour operators provide tour packages and customize tours to meet the needs of tourists. To provide the finest experience to tourists/travellers, tour operators organize tour packages and numerous tourist activities.

4. Travel Information

Tour providers, regardless of their size, have provided travellers with essential travel information. This work is extremely challenging and complex. A tour operator must provide current, accurate, and timely information about destinations, modes of transportation, accommodations, sightseeing, immigration, health and security rules, and numerous permits required to travel in a specific place, among other things.

5. Reservation

It is a very important function of all types of tour operators and travel agencies. Tour operator makes all the reservation by making linkages with the accommodation sector, transport sector, and other entertainment organizations to reserve rooms and seats in cultural programs and transportation.

6. Travel Management

Tour operators manage tours from the beginning to the end of the tour. A tour operator has the responsibility to look after the finer details of a vacation or tour such as hotel, accommodation, meals, conveyance, etc. Tour operators provide travel guides, and escorting services and arrange all travel-related needs and want.

7. Sales and Marketing

Tour operators do sales and marketing of tourist products. Tour operators buy individual travel components, separately and combine them into a tour package, which is sold with their price tag to the public directly. Tour operators do the marketing of tourist destinations and tourism products to attract the attention of the tourists/travellers.

CHAPTER ELEVEN

TOURISM IMPACTS

Life is a journey, not a destination"

– Ralph Waldo Emerson.

TOURISM IMPACTS

Tourist destinations experience both positive and negative effects as a result of tourism. Economic, socio-cultural, and environmental factors are the typical realms of tourism impacts. Tourism's economic effects include greater tax revenue and personal income, higher living standards, and more job opportunities. Interactions between people of different cultural backgrounds, attitudes and behaviours, and relationships with material objects are all examples of sociocultural impacts. Environmental impacts can have both direct and indirect effects, such as habitat degradation, vegetation, air quality, bodies of water, the water table, wildlife, and changes in natural phenomena, as well as increased harvesting of natural resources for food, indirect air and water pollution, and changes in natural phenomena.

ECONOMIC IMPACTS

Expenditure by visitors on tourism experiences, such as beach vacations and theme parks (domestic and foreign), business spending, and capital investment are all subcategories in which tourism has an impact. Tourism's economic contribution is felt in both direct and indirect ways, with direct economic consequences occurring when commodities such as lodging and entertainment, food and beverage services, and retail opportunities are sold. Direct tourism impacts are influenced by residents, visitors, businesses, and various levels of government (local to federal) spending in or around a certain tourism area. Indirect economic impacts of tourism, on the other hand, can be found in private and public investment spending surrounding a tourism offering. This investment may not be directly tied to tourism, yet it nevertheless benefits tourists and local stakeholders.

POSITIVE ECONOMIC IMPACTS OF TOURISM

- Inbound tourism helps to generate revenue from foreign shores.
- Inbound and domestic tourism create job opportunities.
- Inbound and domestic tourism stimulate the development of infrastructure.
- It generates opportunities for small-scale local businesses.

NEGATIVE ECONOMIC IMPACTS OF TOURISM

- Outbound tourism creates economic leakage.
- All types of tourism create a sense of dependency on the customer or economic recession.

- It can also promote parallel economies.
- The revenue earned from the tourism business seldom is beneficial to the local population if the destination has accommodation provided by international hotels.

ENVIRONMENTAL IMPACTS

Ecotourism, nature tourism, wildlife tourism, and adventure tourism take place in environments such as rain forests, high alpine, wilderness, lakes and rivers, coastlines and marine environments, as well as rural villages and coastline resorts. People's desire for more authentic and challenging experiences results in their destinations becoming more remote, to the few remaining pristine and natural environments left on the planet. The positive impact of this can be an increased awareness of environmental stewardship. The negative impact can be the destruction of the very experience that people are seeking. There are direct and indirect impacts, immediate and long-term impacts, and there are impacts that are both proximal and distal to the tourist destination. These impacts can be separated into three categories: facility impacts, tourist activities, and the transit effect.

POSITIVE IMPACTS OF TOURISM ON THE ENVIRONMENT

- It promotes investment in the conservation of natural habitats.
- It thus, in turn, contributes to the stability of the ecosystem.
- In developing countries, it discourages deforestation and over-fishing in large water bodies.
- It contributes to creating awareness of the value of the environment for humans.

POSITIVE IMPACTS OF TOURISM ON THE ENVIRONMENT

- It promotes vandalism and littering.
- It makes way for the destruction of wildlife and vegetation.
- It invites air, and water pollution.
- It creates a large carbon footprint.
- It creates a sense of dependency on natural resources.

SOCIOCULTURAL IMPACTS

The pursuit of authenticity, or the desire to experience a diverse cultural setting in its natural setting, is an essential part of tourism. Although cultural tourism offers chances for understanding and education, it also has negative consequences. It's not just the amount of tourism at work that matters, but also the types of social interactions that take place between the tourist and the host. At the local level, there are three broad effects: the commodification of culture, demonstration effect, and acculturation of another culture.

COMMODIFICATION OF CULTURE

The commodification of culture refers to the use of cultural traditions and artefacts to sell and profit from the local economy. Authors argue that commercialization is unavoidable with the rise of tourism. Commodification has both positive and negative sociocultural effects on culture. One advantage is that it generates revenue and jobs for local artisans who can sell their wares to tourists. Rural tourism is viewed as a "cure" for poverty, as it leads to better transportation and telecommunications in a certain area. Commodification piques tourist interest in traditional arts and social behaviours.

Some researchers, on the other hand, argue that interaction with the secular West destroys pre-tourist cultures. Furthermore, it is claimed that the "development cure," the idea that increasing tourism will spur economic change while strengthening local culture, will lead to a slew of social issues, including drug abuse, crime, pollution, prostitution, social instability, and the spread of capitalist values and consumer culture.

DEMONSTRATION EFFECT

When researchers were looking into the effects of social influences from tourism on local communities, the demonstration effect was introduced. According to the demonstration effect, residents imitate tourist behaviour patterns. The demonstration effect manifests itself for a variety of social, economic, and behavioural reasons. Locals replicate the consumption patterns of individuals higher up the social scale to better their social position, which is one economic and social rationale. Tourism has also been accused of influencing the social conduct of younger residents of a host community, who may emulate visitor behaviour and therefore challenge conventional value systems.

ACCULTURATION

Acculturation is the process of altering one's own culture by drawing from more dominant cultures. The destination community is usually the one that gets acculturated in tourism, and as a result, profound changes in social structure and worldview occur. Acculturation affects societies in one of two ways. When a community absorbs techniques produced by another group, it is known as innovation diffusion; however, cultural adaptation refers to the process of modifying an existing culture rather than the adoption of a new culture.

Acculturation is often seen as a method of modernizing a community and there are many opposing views to the concept of modernization. One argument against modernization is that it contributes to the "homogenization of cultural differences and the decline of traditional societies". This means that communities will advertise their modernity to attract tourists, and will disregard their traditional customs and values. On the other hand, others argue that acculturation and modernization will help traditional communities adjust to a modern world. The idea is that teaching people to adapt will save the community from future extinction.

Printed by Libri Plureos GmbH in Hamburg,
Germany